FOOD LABELING

Politics and Policies in the United States

Edited by
Courtney I.P. Thomas
& Joshua M. Oliver

FOOD LABELING

Politics and Policies in the United States

Edited by
Courtney I.P. Thomas
& Joshua M. Oliver

COMMON GROUND

First published in 2020
as part of the Food Studies Book Imprint
http://doi.org/10.18848/978-1-86335-192-8/CGP (Full Book)

Common Ground Research Networks
2001 South First Street, Suite 202
University of Illinois Research Park
Champaign, IL
61820

Library of Congress Cataloging-in-Publication Data

Names: Thomas, Courtney Irene Powell, editor. | Oliver, Joshua, editor.
Title: Food labeling politics and policies in the United States / edited by
  Courtney I.P. Thomas & Joshua Oliver.
Description: Champaign, IL : Common Ground Research Networks, 2020. |
  Includes bibliographical references. | Summary: "What is included on
  food labels and what is excluded? What are the criteria for "organic"
  foods and who determines that those criteria have been met? Do nutrition
  panels effectively communicate information to consumers? What is the
  difference between "free range" and "cage free," and which should one
  buy if he or she loves eggs and chickens? When a product is labeled as
  "gluten free," has there been some kind of certification process, and
  who can be held accountable if someone dies after eating inaccurately
  labeled food? Those questions are the impetus for this book, which
  delves into related research to find those answers and what those
  answers mean to the U.S. at large"-- Provided by publisher.
Identifiers: LCCN 2019052595 (print) | LCCN 2019052596 (ebook) | ISBN
  9781863351904 (hardback) | ISBN 9781863351911 (paperback) | ISBN
  9781863351928 (pdf)
Subjects: LCSH: Food--Labeling--United States. | Nutrition policy--United
  States.
Classification: LCC TX360.U6 F6836 2020 (print) | LCC TX360.U6 (ebook) |
  DDC 363.8/5610973--dc23
LC record available at https://lccn.loc.gov/2019052595
LC ebook record available at https://lccn.loc.gov/2019052596

Cover Photo Credit: Brittani Musgrove/CGRN

DEDICATION

For Mom and Dad, whose decision to take their first vacation in 20 years afforded me a week without an internet connection, during which I could complete chapter edits with no excuses or distractions.

And for Granny Audrey and Grandpa Lee, in whose home I completed them.

I love you all.

—Courtney I. P. Thomas

For my maternal and paternal grandfathers, Paul and Richard. Thank you for being a constant reminder that hardwork and dedication will lead to success over time, and for providing encouragement every step of the way. Thank you both. I love you.

—Joshua M. Oliver

Table of Contents

PREFACE

In November 2001, I was diagnosed with Celiac Disease and forced to adapt to a completely gluten free diet years before "gluten free" was a food fad or a household term. In the months that followed I became all too acquainted with food labels and found myself fascinated by the information they contained (or, in my case, didn't contain because the inclusion of allergen warnings was still several years out). As my interest in food science and regulation developed, label claims such as "organic," "fair trade," and "non-GMO" led to questions about transparency, accountability, and governance. What is included on food labels and what is excluded? What are the criteria for "organic" foods and who determines that those criteria have been met? Do nutrition panels effectively communicate information to consumers? What is the difference between "free range" and "cage free," and which should I buy if I love eggs and chickens? When a product is labeled as "gluten free," has there been some kind of certification process, and who can be held accountable if I die after eating inaccurately labeled food?

And thus this book was born.

I remain grateful, as ever, to the diverse group of scholars represented by the Common Ground Food Studies Knowledge Community. At our inaugural conference in Las Vegas in 2011, I found the intellectual home I had been seeking. This community represents scholars and practitioners from different academic backgrounds, professions, countries, and polities that comes together annually to share ideas, experiences, and perspectives. Each year at its conferences and continually by way of its peer reviewed journal and book series, Common Ground creates a space for open and honest discussions regarding the most basic, universal, and common human denominator—food—and it does it in a way that encourages mutual respect, collaboration, and the very best of what learning can and should be.

In beginning this project, I had only to remind myself to trust my community and know that it wouldn't let me down. And as you will see in the scholarship reflected in this manuscript, it didn't. Indeed, members of the knowledge community came through, surpassing my expectations and giving generously of their expertise, energies, and research to create this edited volume. It is a privilege to be a part of the Common Ground organization, and to represent it. Thank you to the contributors, Phillip Kalantzis-Cope, the Chief Social Scientist of Common Ground Research Networks, and my research assistant, Josh Oliver. None of this could have been possible without you.

CONTRIBUTORS

Mike Basil (Ph.D., Stanford University) is a Professor of Marketing in the Dhillon School of Business at the University of Lethbridge in Canada. Mike's research is in the areas of advertising, celebrity effects, and social marketing. More recently he has focused on food choice—especially how taste, price, convenience, and nutritional concerns affect consumers, and the importance of hedonic factors such as appearance and freshness on the consumption of fruits and vegetables. He is also interested in the role of experiences in enriching people's lives; this research has examined fine dining, travel, and recreational activities.

Debra Basil, PhD, is a Professor of Marketing and the Director of the Institute for Consumer and Social Well-being at the Dhillon School of Business, University of Lethbridge. Her academic research has focused on societal well-being in various forms. These include social marketing, cause-marketing, nonprofit issues, and volunteerism. Recently she published a textbook on international social marketing cases, together with her co-editors.

Sameer Deshpande (Ph.D., University of Wisconsin-Madison) is an Associate Professor and Acting Director of Social Marketing @ Griffith at Griffith Business School in Griffith University, Australia. Sameer also serves as the Editor-in-Chief of *Social Marketing Quarterly*. Prior to joining Griffith University, Sameer worked at the University of Lethbridge, Canada and National University of Singapore. Sameer conducts research in social marketing. In that regard, he has published and presented in over 100 peer reviewed publications, book chapters, and leading international conferences. Sameer co-authored with Nancy Lee in 2013, *Social Marketing in India*. Over 20 years, Sameer has also trained, taught, advised, and consulted with students, government, corporate, and non-profit organizations in Canada, U.S., Australia, India, and Singapore.

Samantha L. Mosier is an Assistant Professor in the Department of Political Science at East Carolina University (ECU), where she teaches courses on public policy, public administration, leadership, and environmental policy. She is the author of *Creating Organic Standards in U.S. States: The Diffusion of State Organic Food and Agriculture Legislation* and co-author of *Performance Measurement in Sustainability Programs: Lessons from American Cities*. Her research has also appeared in *Food Policy, Environment and Planning C, Environmental Management*, and *International Journal of Public Administration*. Her research focuses on sustainability with particular interest in sustainable food and agriculture and subnational initiatives to protect the environment.

Gina Keel is Associate Professor of Political Science at the State University of New York, Oneonta. She conducts research and writes about environmental, taxation, and social welfare policies. Her analysis of milk labeling cases, "Commercial Free Speech Trumps the Politics of Food Labeling," was published in *First Amendment*

Studies (2014), and she has contributed to *Governing America* (2010), *Encyclopedia of the U.S. Government and the Environment* (2011), and *Class in America* (2007). She has authored manuscripts on tax policy development and teaching cases on environmental policy analysis. At SUNY Oneonta, she developed innovative courses including presidential election campaigns, with student immersion in the New Hampshire primary, and energy science and policy co-taught with a physicist. She helped establish the Sustainability Across the Curriculum initiative on campus and teaches courses in the Environmental Sustainability program. Dr. Keel was awarded the SUNY Chancellor's Award for Excellence in Teaching in 2019 and she received the SEVA Compassionate Service Award in 2015. Dr. Keel earned a B.A. in Political Economy of Industrial Societies from University of California, Berkeley, and a Ph.D. in Politics from Brandeis University, where she was a fellow at the Gordon Public Policy Center. She also worked for civic education organizations, The Freedom Forum and Commonwealth Club of California.

Alissa Bilfield received her PhD in Public Health from Tulane University, her Master of Science in Environment and Development from the London School of Economics and her Bachelor of Arts in Political Science from Vanderbilt University. She is a faculty member at the McGuire Center for Entrepreneurship, Eller School of Management at the University of Arizona. Her research interests include sustainability, food systems and health innovation, supply chain transparency and inclusive entrepreneurship. Her interdisciplinary background includes work and research in the government, nonprofit and academic sectors that has spanned the United States and 14 different countries, ranging from Guatemala to Sri Lanka. Bilfield is also a social entrepreneur herself, having co-founded a food literacy and cooking education nonprofit called The Cookbook Project.

Julia Lapp (PhD, RD) is a Nutritional Anthropologist, Registered Dietitian and Associate Professor of Food and Nutrition at Ithaca College in Ithaca, NY. Her research interests include food consumer decision-making, animal welfare policy, and regional food systems.

Jamille Palacios Rivera (PhD) possesses a doctoral degree in Food and Resource Economics from the University of Florida, Gainesville. She is an Assistant Professor at the University of Missouri, Columbia. She teaches various applied economic courses in the Division of Applied Social Sciences. Her research includes topics related to public policies and corporate social responsibility impacting labor and food markets.

Courtney I. P. Thomas (Ph.D., Virginia Tech) is the Director of Undergraduate Studies and Collegiate Professor in the Department of Political Science at Virginia Tech. Dr. Thomas is the editor of Food Studies: An Interdisciplinary Journal, and a member of the Food Studies Research Network Advisory Board. Her publications include: *In Food We Trust*, University of Nebraska Press, 2014; *Voices of Hunger* (ed.), Common Ground Publishing, 2014; *Political Culture and the Making of*

Modern Nation States, Paradigm Press, 2014; and *International Political Economy: Navigating the Logic Streams, an Introduction* (coauthored with Edward Weisband), Kendall Hunt, 2010

Joshua M. Oliver (B.A., Virginia Tech) earned a BA in Political Science with a concentration in legal studies. Joshua focused his studies in political economics, political violence, and United States public policy. During his undergraduate career, Joshua worked for the Youth Leadership Initiative at the University of Virginia, Spiros Consulting, LLC and the U.S. Department of State Conflict and Stabilization Bureau, and served as a peer mentor and research assistant. Joshua is a consultant for Deloitte.

CHAPTER 1

Processing Nutrition Labels: Effects of Instructions, Health Conditions and Label Length

Michael D. Basil (University of Lethbridge, Canada)
Debra Z. Basil (University of Lethbridge, Canada)
Sameer Deshpande (Griffith University, Australia)

People are faced with a large number of health decisions every day. These decisions may be easy or difficult for a number of reasons including their importance, the quantity of information considered, and time constraints. The research in this chapter examines whether the use of guidelines, personal relevance, and the quantity of information can affect decision quality.

In this case we examine the context of food choice. Nutrition-related diseases such as cardiovascular disease, diabetes, and obesity are increasing at an alarming rate, as are health care costs. Many countries have attempted to improve people's food choices by providing more information to consumers. To this end, food manufacturers provide nutritional information labels on processed and packaged foods (Nutrition Labeling and Education Act [NLEA] 1990). This nutritional information is now part of the shopping experience. As a result, food selection has become a more complex decision (Hasler 2008; Mela 1999).

A critical question is how people use this nutrition information. Nutrition labels are an interesting phenomenon because their use is an active process. That is, the use of nutrition labels requires a combination of factors – motivation, existing knowledge, provided information, and interpretation or processing of that information. This process is similar to McGuire's input/output model of information processing where the source, message, receiver and destination can shape outcomes such as attention, comprehension, and behavior (McGuire 1968; Bull et. al. 2001). In this case, for nutrition labels to affect food choice, the labels need to be attended to and then processed. This process has been shown with other warning labels – to be effective, a long chain of events must occur, including noticing, comprehending, coding, and complying (Zuckerman and Chaiken 1998). For nutrition labels, this is particularly important for those with nutrition-related conditions for whom the relevance of the issue should lead to greater levels of motivation and more real-world significance. The present research seeks to assess whether the provision of guidelines can improve the use of nutritional information labels by people with and without existing health conditions.

THE USE OF NUTRITION LABELS

Research has shown that many people ignore nutrition labels because they feel they are not relevant (Klopp and MacDonald 1981). Ideally, nutrition labels should facilitate decisions for people with relevant health conditions. Importantly, research has shown those interested in health are more likely to use nutrition information (Vyth et. al. 2009). Recent research has suggested that eye-tracking can be used to examine search and attention to nutrition labels (Antúnez et. al. 2015; Bialkova and van Trijp 2010; Bialkova and van Trijp 2011). This research can provide insights into what gets attended to and what does not, but to date it has not examined what kind of people pay attention to what kinds of information, or if it has any effect on their choices.

Studies have also examined the outcomes of nutrition information. These typically make use of replies on self-reports on label use and food choice. One study found that individuals report altering the frequency they purchase foods based on nutrition label information (ADA 1997). Another study has shown that people have more favorable attitudes and higher purchase intentions toward products with favorable nutrition information (Kozup, Creyer, and Burton 2003). Still other research has demonstrated that reading nutrition labels is associated with higher quality diets (Satia, Galanko, and Neuhouser 2005). In sum, research suggests that nutrition labels can be beneficial to the people who choose to use them and know how to interpret the labels, but does not indicate how the information is processed by most customers.

Other research has examined how consumers use nutrition information. Barone et. al. (1996) found that "daily values" can serve as a reference point to guide consumers' interpretation of nutrition information. Other research has demonstrated that consumers tend to focus on reducing consumption of "bad" things such as fat and sodium (Balasubramanian and Cole 2002; Berning et. al. 2010). However, some research suggests that many consumers have difficulty interpreting these food labels, especially older consumers and those with less education (Byrd-Bredbenner, Wong, and Cottee 2000; Cowburn and Stockley 2005). Unfortunately, older consumers are more likely to have more nutrition-related diseases.

Nutrition labels are particularly relevant with two of the most prevalent nutrition-related health concerns in North America: cardiovascular disease (CVD) and diabetes, since both have important nutritional factors (Franz et. al. 2002; Hooper et. al. 2001). However, little research has examined the use of nutrition labels by people with health conditions, despite the practical importance of this question. An examination of how people with nutritional concerns process nutrition labels may help us better understand individuals with health problems or even design labels for maximum effectiveness.

The question of existing knowledge and effort is important when considering the nutrition facts panel, as it contains a good deal of information. It is important to understand if shortcuts can be used and whether this can affect the quality of decisions. Consistent with the question, some research has demonstrated that the use of nutrition labels follows a rational model where people who are more interested in nutrition are more likely to use the labels (Chu, Frongillo, Jones, and Kaye 2009; Guthrie et. al. 1995).

COGNITIVE PROCESSING THEORIES

One foundation of cognitive psychology is that people's ability to process information is limited. As a result of this limitation, providing too much information can reduce decision quality (Jones, Schipper, and Holzworth 1978). One way to reduce effort requirements is to use shortcuts or "heuristics" to guide decisions (Tversky and Kahneman 1974). People employ these shortcuts when needed and, by doing so, can reduce the time required to make a decision (Lurie 2004). Research has shown that one commonly used strategy is filtering through incoming information and ignoring anything deemed "irrelevant" to one's personal needs (Celsi and Olson 1988).

Health concerns are also expected to serve as a decision guide heuristic, focusing the respondents' attention on some of this information and allowing them to ignore other information. Research suggests that using appropriate decision guides can improve the efficiency of decision making (Gigerenzer and Todd 1999; Payne, Bettman, and Johnson 1991; Scheibehenne, Miesler, and Todd 2007; Thorngate 1980). The use of guidelines may improve the handling of nutrition labels to best benefit food choice decisions.

Bearing this information in mind, this chapter examines the following hypotheses:

H1: People will make more appropriate decisions for their health concerns with decision guidelines than without.

Many countries including the U.S., Canada, and the E.U. allow either short or longer nutrition labels (Cowburn and Stockley 2005). In North America this is at the discretion of the manufacturer; in the E.U. the longer labels are required to support any health claim. These longer labels can be three times longer. The quantity of nutrition information is expected to affect the difficulty of the decisions. The principle of "cognitive economy" (e.g. Feldman and Lynch 1988; Wyer and Srull 1986) suggests that people tend to conserve their cognitive resources and require motivation to use those resources. This suggests that people may be less likely to process all the information on extended nutrition labels unless they have some specific motivation. The additional information provided by extended labels may be ignored as an act of cognitive economy. One important bias is that a focus on less relevant information may shift focus away from the most important elements of the label toward secondary components, maintaining a relatively consistent amount of cognitive processing. This potential shift in focus could reduce decision quality, as secondary information gains precedence over primary information.

Given the nature of cognitive economy, as evidence suggests too much information can reduce decision quality, perhaps even "overload" a person (Malhotra 1984), longer labels could lead to a detrimental shift in focus. An increase in the amount of information presented with no increase in available time or motivation may lead individuals to skim all available information, precluding them from thoroughly processing any of it. Alternatively, longer labels may lead people to shift their focus from primary to secondary information, again suggesting that longer nutrition labels may reduce decision quality (Gigerenzer and Todd 1999). This leads to the following hypothesis:

> *H2: People will make more appropriate decisions for their health concerns with shorter nutrition labels than with longer nutrition labels.*

Another decision heuristic that can be employed is the quick elimination of alternatives. "Negativity bias" is a heuristic that finds ways to eliminate choices. Herr, Kardes, and Kim (1989) found that people often put more weight on negative information than positive information in making judgments. That is, people may eliminate a food choice that is slightly higher in fat even though it is better in other aspects such as sodium and fiber. When trying to identify the conditions under which the negativity effect operates, Ahluwalia (2002) found that the effect is most likely when consumers attempt to reduce risk. In the case of nutrition information, those with CVD were historically advised to limit their fat intake (especially saturated and trans fats) and sodium intake. Those with diabetes were advised to reduce their carbohydrates but increase their fiber intake. Because eliminating options from consideration sets is likely an effective strategy in situations where many judgments must be made, it is likely that consumers will be likely to resort to heuristics that immediately rule out choices.

> *H3: People will put more focus on minimizing detrimental components such as fat than on maximizing beneficial components such as fiber.*

Research on heuristics suggests that guidelines may help people to sift through large amounts of information, but such strategies necessarily mean that some information will receive more attention while other information receives less attention. Specifically, focal information receives more attention, while non-focal information receives less attention. An important process that enables the use of shortcuts is the use of focal versus non-focal attention so that consciousness is directed at some items and away from others (Posner 2004). This process involves the selection of some information at the expense of other information. For example, when people are focused on reducing fat, they may inadvertently increase other non-beneficial components such as sodium or reduce beneficial nutrients such as fiber.

This argument is consistent with the notion of priming. Accessibility helps to determine how new information is encoded, and how it later influences judgment (Srull and Wyer 1979). When certain cognitions are activated in working memory, they temporarily have a disproportionate impact over the nature and content of cognitive processing (Feldman and Lynch 1988). We propose that directing individuals' attention to focal information may follow this route; drawing attention to key health issues activates those concepts, which may divert attention from other potentially relevant health issues.

> *H4: People will make decisions using focal information that will sometimes be at the expense of non-focal information.*

PILOT TEST

Personal relevance is an important determinant of how effective people are at gleaning information from nutrition labels (Jacoby, Chestnut, and Silberman 1977; Moorman 1996). To test that, this study examined if providing simple guidelines in the form of nutritional instructions could improve people's decision choices. That is, when people are provided with simple nutritional instructions (Taylor and Brower 2004), can they apply this as a heuristic to focus on particular information?

Methods

For this study, a 3 (health concern: diabetes, heart disease, no health concern) x 3 (nutrition label: standard U.S. label, standard Canadian label, extended U.S. label) x 2 (counterbalancing variable: order of presentation) between-subjects experiment was conducted with 196 undergraduate students. They were given $5 as compensation. The gender distribution was 45% female and 55% male (n=88 and 106 respectively). Students were predominantly in the 18-to-25-year-old range, representing 84% of the sample (n=162). Responses to height and weight questions were used to calculate each respondent's body mass index (BMI). The average BMI was 23 (a BMI of 25 or more indicates overweight).

Stimuli. Nutrition facts panels allowed respondents to choose from competing products. This information was taken from real food products to enhance the external validity of the study (Nutri-Facts 2006). A search of the database identified product categories that had options clearly differing on sugar and fat content. For each product category selected, three different products were identified by the researchers: one that would be the best choice for those with diabetes, one that would be the best choice for those with heart disease, and one product that generally fell between these two. Using real product labels resulted in constraints—sometimes the chosen products did not fit the criteria perfectly, but this was deemed acceptable because of the external validity gained by using actual product labels.

Manipulations. Three independent variables were manipulated. *Nutrition instructions* involved a fictitious doctor's letter with nutritional instructions intended to mimic suggestions to people with a specific health condition. Respondents were randomly assigned to one of three nutrition instructions. One indicated a family history of diabetes, and that the respondent was at risk of contracting diabetes. They were instructed to eat fewer simple sugars and more fiber. Sugar was used rather than carbohydrates to simplify the decision process and make it equivalent to the heart disease instructions (the instruction to avoid sugar was commonly used in the past, Franz et. al. 2002). The second set of nutrition instructions indicated a family history and risk of heart disease. These respondents were instructed to eat a diet low in saturated and trans fats. The third nutrition instruction condition indicated generally good health. Respondents in this condition were simply encouraged to "eat right." Respondents were told to keep these nutrition instructions in mind when making food choices during the study. [The letters are presented in Appendix A.]

The second independent variable was the type of *nutrition label* that the respondent viewed. One group viewed the standard Canadian nutrition label, another group viewed the standard American nutrition label, and a third group viewed an extended American nutrition label which included trans-fat information. These label formats were chosen to vary information level and familiarity. [Examples of nutrition labels are presented in Appendix B.]

The third independent variable was a non-theoretical *ordering* variable. Two ordering conditions were used to control for the possible impact of order of presentation.

Procedure. The study was run online, with individuals assigned to their own computer and randomly assigned to conditions. Respondents first viewed the nutritional instructions. They were then given a list of foods representing typical packaged or processed foods for one day and informed that they were to make decisions for each. They were asked to record their start time using a wall clock in the room. Respondents were then shown three different nutrition labels in each of nine food categories (yogurt, cereal, potato chips, bread, ham, cookies, soup, frozen entree, and pie) and asked to choose one from each. Respondents repeated this procedure for all nine product categories. They were asked to spend as much time on the decision as they would if they were really grocery shopping. After their final product decision, they were asked to record their end time. Outside the lab they were then given $5 and a feedback sheet informing them of the purpose of the study.

Dependent measures. To assess the quality of food choice, a sum of nutritional elements for the foods selected was calculated across the nine product decisions. The calories, grams of saturated fat, sugar, and fiber, and milligrams of sodium were summed as dependent variables.

Results

Manipulations. To assess the effect of the instructions on decision quality (H1), respondents' selected food choices were assessed. Respondents made food selections appropriate to their nutritional instructions[1]. Nutritional instruction was a significant predictor of saturated fat (F [2, 193] = 6.2, p = .002, eta^2 = .06), sugar (F [2, 193] = 6.1, p = .003, eta^2 = .06), and fiber (F [2, 193] = 10.6, p < .001, eta^2 = .10). This result is shown in Table 1.

Table 1: Count of Calories, Saturated Fat, Sodium, Sugar, and Fiber of Selections by Condition

	Calories	Saturated Fat	Sodium	Sugar	Fiber
Healthy Instructions	1468 (145)	6.1 (2.8)	3966 (328)	71.1 (28.8)	20.9 (7.0)
Diabetes Instructions	1451 (128)	7.2 (3.2)	3899 (444)	53.9 (33.0)	24.8 (8.0)

---

[1] Of the 9 choices, on average 2.4 represented the low sugar/high fiber option, and 4.1 were low fat choices. On average 4.2 of the options represented the best choice for the respondent's nutritional instructions, for an average accuracy rate of 47%. For comparison, an individual would be expected to be 33% accurate (1 of 3) due to chance.

CVD	1437	5.3	3831	67.0	19.0
Instructions	(145)	(3.1)	(386)	(25.5)	(6.7)
Significance	.382	.002	.146	.003	<.001

Note: Mean number of calories, grams of fat, sugar, and fiber and mg of sodium (Standard deviation in parentheses).

Hypothesis tests. The effect of label length on decision quality (H2) was tested. Respondents' consistency score relative to their nutritional instructions served as the dependent variable. Nutrition instructions, nutrition label, and order of presentation served as factors, BMI and gender as covariates. The results indicated that the form of the nutrition label did not matter (p > .10)—extended nutrition labels did not lead to poorer decisions.

Examining the effect of minimization versus maximization guidelines (H3), instructions were significant (F [1, 162] = 7.2, p < .01). Respondents with the heart disease instructions selected low fat options significantly more than respondents with the diabetes instructions selected the low sugar/high fiber option (M = 4.8 vs. 3.6 respectively).

Discussion

These results support the value of instructions on food choices—people made more appropriate decisions when provided with nutrition guidelines. Importantly, the form of the label did not matter. Familiarity did not affect decision quality. Length of label also had no effect on decision quality, suggesting extended labels are not problematic.

MAIN EXPERIMENT

The pilot study demonstrates that university students can use nutritional instructions to guide appropriate food choices. However, the question of what information people typically use and how effective they are at using it to make nutrition decisions remains.

The final experiment improved on the pilot study in five important ways. First, a non-student sample was used. This is important because students may be more accustomed to sifting through information and taking multiple-choice examinations which are similar to the study task, and therefore better suited to this sort of task. Second, real pre-existing health conditions were examined where existing strategies probably apply. This was done by restricting the sample to respondents over 40, examining health concerns such as diabetes and CVD. Third, rather than simply inferring importance from decisions, respondents were directly asked about the importance they placed on nutrients when making decisions, which served as a direct measure of guidelines. Fourth, this study used the broader health condition of cardiovascular disease (CVD) rather than heart disease. Fifth, the design was simplified by using only short and long U.S. labels. Since the study only used the U.S. labels and used an American sample, respondents were exposed to a familiar label format which eliminated any possibility of novelty effects.

Method. A 3 (health concern: none, diabetes, CVD) x 2 (nutrition label: standard, extended) x 2 (nutrition instructions: yes, no) between-subjects experiment was conducted online. Several questions were also asked following the experimental portion of the study.

Respondents. Respondents were part of a Zoomerang on-line research panel (see http://www.zoomerang.com). For participating, each respondent received points which can be accumulated and exchanged for gifts. An invitation to participate in the on-line study was sent to 2,200 Zoomerang panel members over 40. A total of 977 panel members began the study (44%), 177 terminated before completion (18%), resulting in 800 completed surveys (82% of those who began the study).

A total of 486 respondents were classified as "no health concern" in that they self-reported neither diabetes nor CVD. A total of 165 self-reported having diabetes, and 90 self-reported having CVD. Fifty-nine reported both diabetes and CVD, so were excluded from the analyses because determination of best choices for these individuals was less clear. This left a total of 741 valid cases.

The gender distribution was 46% female and 54% male (n = 367 and 425 respectively, 14 missing). The average respondent age was 58 years old. Responses to height and weight questions were used to calculate each respondent's body mass index (BMI). The average BMI was 30 (for reference, a BMI of 25 or more indicates an overweight person). The mean and median education level for this sample was an Associates (2 year) college degree. The mean and median income range was between $50,000 and $74,999.

Manipulations. Respondents were randomly assigned to one of two label conditions: standard or extended labels. The research used the nutritional instructions as pilot tested. Half of each group was randomly assigned to receive nutrition instructions, and half received none. For those receiving the instructions, the content of their instructions depended upon their self-reported health condition. People with diabetes received instructions encouraging them to reduce their sugar intake and increase their fiber intake. Those with CVD received instructions encouraging them to reduce saturated fats and sodium. Those with neither diabetes nor CVD (no health concern condition) received a letter encouraging them to try to eat a healthy diet by reducing fat and increasing fiber.

Procedure. Respondents first viewed an introductory and informed consent statement. They then indicated any health conditions such as diabetes and CVD to assign them to an appropriate health condition. They were randomly assigned to the nutrition instructions condition and label length condition.

As in the pilot test, respondents selected food options from a pre-set menu. For each of the nine menu items, they viewed three different nutrition labels, and selected one option for each. The same nutrition labels used in the pilot test were used here. Following these choices respondents were then asked a variety of survey questions.

Measures

Guidelines. Survey questions asked how important a variety of nutrients were (calories, fat, carbohydrates, sugar, fiber, and sodium), on a scale from 1 to 7, anchored by unimportant and very important, to assess importance in making their choices.

    Analysis. SPSS's multiple linear regression procedure was used with mean substitution in the case of missing data. These mean substitutions were necessary for BMI (22 respondents), education level (9 respondents), income (60 respondents), and sex (14 respondents).

Results

Manipulation check. To assess the effects of existing health conditions and nutrition instructions, questions were asked about how important each nutrient was to the respondent's decision. Responses were made on 7-point Likert scales anchored by "unimportant" at 1 and "very important" at 7. To test the effect of the instructions, an ANOVA was used to compare the differences between the focal nutrients as the dependent variable and nutrition instructions and health concern as independent variables. Measures are shown in Table 2.

Table 2: Nutrtitional Focus by Experimental Condition

	Calories	Saturated Fat	Sodium	Sugar	Fiber
Healthy	5.0	5.5	5.2	4.6	4.9
No instructions	(1.5)	(1.6)	(1.7)	(1.9)	(1.7)
Healthy	5.0	5.7	5.3	4.8	5.2
Instructions	(1.6)	(1.4)	(1.7)	(1.6)	(1.6)
Diabetes	4.8	5.0	5.0	6.1	5.0
No instructions	(1.5)	(1.6)	(1.8)	(1.4)	(1.7)
Diabetes	4.9	5.1	5.1	6.4	5.5
Instructions	(1.5)	(1.6)	(1.7)	(6.4)	(1.5)
CVD	4.4	5.9	5.8	4.5	4.9
No instructions	(1.7)	(1.4)	(1.6)	(1.6)	(1.9)
CVD	4.9	5.9	5.9	4.4	5.0
Instructions	(1.4)	(1.4)	(1.5)	(1.7)	(1.6)
Significance	.290	<.001	.02	<.001	.012

Note: Mean reported importance on 1 (unimportant) to 7 (extremely important) scale

The effect of nutrition instructions was significant (F $[1, 739]$ = 7.0, p < .01). Respondents receiving nutrition instructions placed more importance on the nutrients in the instructions relative to the other nutrients, indicating the manipulation was successful. Consistent with their instructions, the results show that existing health conditions were primarily responsible for people's nutritional focus relevant to their condition with saturated fats (F $[2, 738]$ = 14.2, p < .001), trans fats (F $[2, 738]$ = 9.6, p < .001), sugars (F $[2, 738]$ = 8.4, p < .001), and fiber (F $[1, 739]$ = 6.4, p = .012).

    Univariate results. Across all respondents, the most frequently reported naturally-occurring guidelines people reported using were fat (54%) followed by sodium (32%), calories (30%), carbohydrates (24%) and sugar (22%). The guidelines changed slightly after the nutrition instructions. An analysis of guideline use showed that people reported using an average of 1.6 guidelines in the "no letter" condition (compared to 1.4 in the nutrition instructions condition).

Hypothesis Tests

To test H1 on the effect of health concerns, an ANOVA with the nutritional totals of the food selected served as the dependent variable. Health condition, nutrition instructions, and label length were factors and BMI, sex, age, income, and education were covariates. Consistent with H1, health condition significantly predicted saturated fat (F [2, 738] = 17.3, p < .001), sodium (F [2, 738] = 7.5, p = .001), and sugar (F [2, 738] = 103, p < .001) in food selection. With regard to the instructions, exposure to the letter increased fiber in food selections (F [2, 738] = 102, p < .001). No other variables were significant (all p > .05). The means are reported in Table 3.

Table 3: Count of Calories, Saturated Fat, Sodium, Sugar, and Fiber of Selections by Condition

	Calories	Saturated Fat	Sodium	Sugar	Fiber
Healthy	1408	5.7	3620	60.8	18.4
No instructions	(150)	(2.5)	(497)	(32)	(6.9)
Healthy	1391	5.1	3677	64.0	19.2
Instructions	(132)	(2.6)	(478)	(31)	(7.1)
Diabetes	1400	7.3	3636	30.0	19.1
No instructions	(112)	(2.7)	(378)	(27)	(7.6)
Diabetes	1400	7.8	3660	26.6	19.9
Instructions	(132)	(3.2)	(416)	(27)	(8.2)
CVD	1400	4.9	3434	70.2	18.0
No instructions	(147)	(2.7)	(642)	(28)	(7.0)
CVD	1367	4.6	3525	62.5	19.3
Instructions	(99)	(1.9)	(561)	(28)	(7.6)
Significance	.41	<.001	.02	<.001	.46

Note: Mean number of calories, grams of fat, sugar, and fiber and mg of sodium (Standard deviation in parentheses).

To assess H2, whether extended label length harmed decision accuracy, an ANOVA was run where consistency with the provided guideline served as the dependent variable. Health condition, nutrition instructions, and label condition served as factors. BMI, sex, age, income, and education served as covariates. Label length did not affect food choice, failing to support H2 (F [1, 739] = 1.3, p > .7). Extended nutrition labels did not impair decision making. This is consistent with the findings of the pilot study.

H3 predicted that people would place more emphasis on nutrients they were trying to minimize than nutrients they were seeking to maximize. To assess this, paired samples t-tests were conducted on the importance ratings for the diabetes and the no health concern condition respondents who received nutrition instructions, as these were the two conditions instructed to maximize fiber. In both conditions, fiber was rated as less important to their food choice decisions than the nutrient they were told to minimize (sugar for people with diabetes, saturated and trans fats for no health concern individuals). For people with diabetes, the average difference in importance weightings for fiber compared to sugar was 1.1 (t [79] = 5.4, p < .001), suggesting that sugar played a significantly larger role in their food choice decisions than did fiber. For no health concern individuals, the average difference in importance of fiber compared to saturated fat was .58 (t [245] = 5.6, p < .001), suggesting greater importance for saturated fat, supporting our prediction that greater importance was placed on minimizing sugar and fats than on maximizing fiber.

H4 predicted that the use of guidelines would result in better choices for focal nutrients than for non-focal nutrients. As predicted, focus reduced the saturated fat, sodium, sugar, and fiber content of their choices. These effects are shown in Table 4.

Table 4: Effect of Provided Guidelines on Saturated Fat, Sodium, Sugar, and Fiber of Selections

	Saturated Fat	Sodium	Sugar	Fiber
Focal	4.8	3526	26.6	24.2
	(2.5)	(561)	(27)	(7.5)
Non-focal	7.8	3679	64.0	17.4
	(3.2)	(469)	(31)	(7.7)
F	114	8.9	142	115
Significance	<.001	.003	<.001	<.001

Discussion

These results provide insight into how the use of nutrition labels can be improved. First, because respondents chose appropriate options at a rate higher than chance (42 versus 33%), they show that nutrition labels can help people make food selections that are more appropriate for existing health conditions. Second, they demonstrate that when people are given nutritional instructions on what to look for, this further improves their ability to select foods. Third, the results of this experiment are consistent with the notion of heuristics. When people make use of imagined or real health conditions to choose foods, they do so in ways consistent with their health conditions, and when specific nutritional guidelines are provided, individuals also appear to use them in making food choices, but they do so at the expense of other information.

GENERAL DISCUSSION

The results of these studies demonstrate the importance of focal attention in nutrition information use. The pilot test using a student sample demonstrates that when instructions are provided, people can use this information to make healthier food selections. The results of the experiment with a mature adult sample demonstrate that people with nutrition-related health conditions can use nutrition labels to select more appropriate food, whether this was using existing strategies or manipulated nutrition instructions. Therefore, we conclude that the labels are helpful for those with health conditions (Chu et. al. 2009; Glanz et. al. 1995; Miller et. al. 2002; Temple et. al. 2010). These findings run counter to suggestions that consumers are confused by nutrition information (Hasler 2008).

The results also suggest that the provision of specific guidelines to process nutrition labels can be beneficial. First, extended labels did not hinder decision making quality in either of the experiments. So these findings suggest that people are as accurate with extended nutrition facts panels as they are with short labels. This does not support the notion of information "overload" in the form of reduced decision quality. Second, the consistency between the nutritional instructions and effects of health conditions suggest that people with health conditions are likely using processes very similar to those provided in the nutrition instructions.

How can people be as accurate with longer labels? The explanation is that people are using strategies to limit the amount of information they process (Gigerenzer and Todd 1999; Lurie 2004). In the case of nutrition labels, the consistency between the pilot test and main experiment suggest that people are looking at a few key nutrients. These findings are consistent with the heuristic use found in previous research on NLEA labels as well (e.g., Balasubramanian and Cole 2002; Barone et. al. 1996; Berning et. al. 2010). Importantly, this study demonstrates the cost of this approach—ignoring non-focal information. Our analyses comparing food choices on focal versus non-focal nutrients demonstrates that this limited focus can result in non-focal nutrient choices that are worse when a focal guideline was used.

These results have implications for processing health information in general. When dealing with a lot of information, people will often employ shortcuts. And when they use these shortcuts, they can often make decisions with some focal information, but this is at the expense of information outside their focus. This study demonstrates that the fast and frugal approach (Gigerenzer and Todd 1999) has its limitations.

REFERENCES

Ahluwalia, Rohini. "How prevalent is the negativity effect in consumer environments?" *Journal of Consumer Research* 29 (2002): 270-281.

Antúnez, Lucía, Ana Giménez, Alejandro Maiche, and Gastón Ares. "Influence of interpretation aids on attentional capture, visual processing, and understanding of front-of-package nutrition labels." *Journal of Nutrition Education and Behavior* 47, no.4 (2015): 292-299.

Balasubramanian, Siva K., and Catherine Cole. "Consumers' search and use of nutrition information: The challenge and promise of the nutrition labeling and education act." *Journal of Marketing* 66 (2002): 112-127.

Barone, Michael J., Randall L. Rose, Kenneth C. Manning, and Paul W. Miniard. "Another look at the impact of reference information on consumer impressions of nutrition information." *Journal of Public Policy and Marketing* 15 (1996): 55-62.

Berning, Joshua P., Hayley H. Chouinard, Kenneth C. Manning, Jill J. McCluskey, and David E. Sprott. "Identifying consumer preferences for nutrition information on grocery store shelf labels." *Food Policy* 35, no.5 (2010): 429-436.

Bialkova, Svetlana, and Hans van Trijp. "What determines consumer attention to nutrition labels?." *Food Quality and Preference* 21 (2010): 1042-1051.

———. "An efficient methodology for assessing attention to and effect of nutrition information displayed front-of-pack." *Food Quality and Preference* 22 (2011): 592-601.

Bull, Fiona C., Cheryl L. Holt, Marshall W. Kreuter, Eddie M. Clark, and Darcy Scharff. "Understanding the effects of printed health education materials: which features lead to which outcomes?" *Journal of Health Communication* 6 (2001): 265-279.

Byrd-Bredbenner, Carol, Angela Wong, and Peta Cottee. "Consumer understanding of US and EU nutrition labels." *British Food Journal* 102 (2000): 615–629.

Celsi, Richard L., and Jerry C. Olson. "The role of involvement in attention and comprehension processes." *Journal of Consumer Research* 15 (1988): 210-224.

CDC Centers for Disease Control and Prevention 2011, March 16. Deaths: Preliminary data for 2009. *National Vital Statistics Report: 594.*

Chu, Yong H., Edward A. Frongillo, Sonya J. Jones, and Gail L. Kaye. "Improving patrons' meal selections through the use of point-of-selection nutrition labels." *American Journal of Public Health* 99, no.11 (2009): 2001-2005.

Cowburn, Gill, and Lynn Stockley. "Consumer understanding and use of nutrition labeling: A systematic review." *Public Health Nutrition* 8 (2005): 21-28.

Feldman, Jack M., and John G. Lynch. "Self-generated validity and other effects of measurement on belief, attitude, intention, and behavior." *Journal of Applied Psychology* 73, no. 3 (1988): 421-435.

Franz, Marion J., John P. Bantle, Christine A. Beebe, John D. Brunzell, Jean-Louis Chiasson, Abhimanyu Garg, Lea Ann Holzmeister, B. Hoogwerf, E. Mayer-Davis, A. D. Mooradian, J. Q. Purnell and M. Wheeler. "Evidence-based nutrition principles and recommendations for the treatment and prevention of diabetes and related complications." *Diabetes Care* 25 (2002): 148-198.

Gigerenzer, Gerd, and Peter M. Todd. "Fast and frugal heuristics." In *Simple Heuristics That Make Us Smart,* edited by G. Grenzer and P. M. Todd, 3-34. New York: Oxford (1994).

Glanz, Karen, Becky Lankenau, Susan Foerster, Sally Temple, Rebecca Mullis, and Thomas Schmid. "Environmental and policy approaches to cardiovascular disease prevention through nutrition: Opportunities for state and local action." *Health Education Quarterly* 22 (1995): 512-527.

Guthrie, Joanne F., Jonathan J. Fox, Linda E. Cleveland, and Susan Welsh. "Who uses nutrition labeling, and what effect does label use have on diet quality?" *Journal of Nutrition Education,* 27, no. 4 (1995): 163-172.

Hasler, Claire M. "Health claims in the United States: An aid to the public or a source of confusion?" *Journal of Nutrition,* 138 (2008): 1216S-1220S.

Herr, Paul M., Frank Kardes and John Kim. "Effects of word-of-mouth and product-attribute information on persuasion: An accessibility-diagnostic perspective." *Journal of Consumer Research,* 17 (1991): 454-462.

Hooper, Lee, Carolyn D. Summerbell, Julian PT Higgins, Rachel L. Thompson, Nigel E. Capps, George Davey Smith, Rudolph A. Riemersma, and Shah Ebrahim. "Dietary fat intake and prevention of cardiovascular disease: A review." *British Medical Journal,* 322 (2001): 757-763.

Jacoby, Jacob, Robert W. Chestnut and William Silberman.. "Consumer use and comprehension of nutrition information." *Journal of Consumer Research,* 4 (1977): 119-128.

Jones, David P., Lowell M. Schipper, and R. James Holzworth. "Effects of amount of information on decision strategies." *Journal of General Psychology,* 98, no. 2 (1978): 281-294.

Klopp, Pamela and Maurice McDonald. "Nutrition labels: An exploratory study of consumer reasons for nonuse. " *Journal of Consumer Affairs,* 15 (1981): 301-316.

Lurie, Nicolas H. "Decision making in information-rich environments: The role of information structure." *Journal of Consumer Research,* 30 (2004): 473-486.

Malhotra, Naresh K. "Reflections on the information overload paradigm in consumer decision making." *Journal of Consumer Research,* 10, no. 4 (1984): 436-440.

McGuire, William J. "Personality and attitude change: An information processing theory." In *Psychological Foundations of Attitudes,* edited by A. Greenwald, T. Brock and T. Ostrom, 171-196. New York: Academic Press (1968).

Mela, David J. "Food choice and intake: The human factor." *Proceedings of the Nutrition Society,* 58 (1999): 513-526.

Miller, Carla K., Lesley Edwards, Grace Kissling, and Laurel Sanville. "Nutrition education improves metabolic outcomes among older adults with diabetes mellitus: Results from a randomized controlled trial." *Preventative Medicine,* 34 (2002): 252-259.

Moorman, Christine. "A quasi experiment to assess the consumer and information determinants of nutrition information processing activities: The case of the Nutrition Labeling and Education Act." *Journal of Public Policy and Marketing,* 15 (1996): 28-44.

Neuhouser, Marian L., Alan R. Kristal, and Ruth E. Patterson. "Use of food nutrition labels is associated with lower fat intake." *Journal of the American Dietetic Association,* 99 (1999): 45-53.

Nutri-Facts 2006. *http://www.nutri-facts.com/search.php.* Accessed on-line April 14, 2008 and May 26, 2011.

Nutrition Education and Labeling Act of 1990. United States Public Law 101-535, 104, Statute 2353.

Payne, J., J. R. Bettman, and E. J. Johnson. "Consumer decision making." In *Handbook of Consumer Behavior,* edited by Thomas S. Robertson and Harold K. Kassarjian, 50-84. Englewood Cliffs, NJ: Prentice Hall (1991).

Posner, Michael I. *The Cognitive Neuroscience of Attention.* New York: Guildford Press (2004).

Satia, Jessie A., Joseph A. Galanko, and Marian L. Neuhouser. "Food nutrition label use is associated with demographic, behavioral, and psychosocial factors and dietary intake among African Americans in North Carolina." *Journal of the American Dietetic Association,* 105 (2005): 392-402.

Scheibehenne, Benjamin, Linda Miesler, and Peter M. Todd. "Fast and frugal food choices: Uncovering individual decision heuristics." *Appetite,* 49 (2007): 578-589.

Srull, Thomas K. and Robert S. Wyer. "The role of category accessibility in the interpretation of information about persons: Some determinants and implications." *Journal of Personality and Social Psychology,* 37, no. 10 (1979): 1660-1672.

Teisl, Mario F., and Alan S. Levy. "Does nutrition labeling lead to healthier eating?" *Journal of Food Distribution Research,* 3, no. 28(1997): 19-26.

Temple, Jennifer L, Karena Johnson, Kelly Recupero and Heather Suders. "Nutrition labels decrease energy intake in adults consuming lunch in the laboratory." *Journal of the American Dietetic Association*, 110, no.7 (2010): 1094-1097.

Thorngate, Warren. Efficient decision heuristics. *Behavioral Science*, 25 (1980): 219–225.

Tversky, Amos and Daniel Kahneman. "Judgment under uncertainty: Heuristics and biases." *Science*, 185 (1974): 1124-1130.

Vyth, Ellis L., Ingrid HM Steenhuis, Sanne F. Mallant, Zinzi L. Mol, Johannes Brug, Marcel Temminghoff, Gerda I. Feunekes, Léon Jansen, Hans Verhagen, and Jacob C. Seidell. "A front-of-pack nutrition logo: a quantitative and qualitative process evaluation in the Netherlands." *Journal of Health Communication*, 14 (2009): 631-645.

Wyer, Robert S. Jr., and Thomas K. Srull. "Human cognition in its social context." *Psychological Review*, 93 (1986): 322-359.

Zuckerman, Adam and Shelly Chaiken. "A heuristic-systematic processing analysis of the effectiveness of product warning labels." *Psychology & Marketing*, 15 (1988): 621-642.

APPENDIX A:

Doctor's Letters

Control:

Dear Patient: This letter is a follow-up to your recent office visit. As we discussed, the results of your annual physical examination were generally fine. One of the best ways to maintain good health is to eat a healthy diet. Currently three of the top five leading causes of death are related to poor eating habits. I encourage you to begin watching your diet now, by reducing SATURATED/TRANS FATS and increasing FIBER. We will check your status again next year at your annual physical examination.

Sincerely,
Dr. Smith

CVD:

Dear Patient: This letter is a follow-up to your recent office visit. As we discussed, the results of your annual physical examination indicated cardiovascular disease (CVD). CVD is extremely serious, and in fact it is one of the top five leading causes of death. One of the best ways to manage your CVD is to eat a healthy diet, low in SATURATED/TRANS FATS and low in SODIUM. I encourage you to begin watching your diet now, in order to avoid future trouble. We will check your status again next year at your annual physical examination.

Sincerely,
Dr. Smith

Diabetes:

Dear Patient:
This letter is a follow-up to your recent office visit. As we discussed, the results of your annual physical examination indicated diabetes. Diabetes is extremely serious, and in fact it is one of the top five leading causes of death. One of the best ways to manage your diabetes is to eat a healthy diet, low in SUGARS and high in FIBER. I encourage you to begin watching your diet now, in order to avoid future trouble. We will check your status again next year at your annual physical examination.

Sincerely,
Dr. Smith

APPENDIX B:

Sample Nutrition Labels

Yogurt: A

Nutrition Facts
Serving Size 100 g
Servings Per Container 1
Amount Per Serving

Calories 94

		% Daily Value*
Total Fat 0 g		0%
Saturated 0 g		1%
+ Trans		
Polyunsaturated 0.0 g		
Omega-6 Polyunsaturated		
Omega-3 Polyunsaturated		
Monounsaturated 0.1 g		
Cholesterol 2 mg		1%
Sodium 58 mg		2%
Potassium 194 mg		6%
Total Carbohydrate 19 g		6%
Dietary Fibre 0 g		0%
Soluble Fibre		
Insoluble Fibre		
Sugars 19 g		
Sugar Alcohols		
Starch 0 g		
Protein 4 g		

Vitamin A	0%	Vitamin C	1%
Calcium	15%	Iron	0%
Vitamin D	0%	Vitamin E	0%
Vitamin K	1%	Thiamine	3%
Riboflavin	11%	Niacin	1%
Vitamin B₆	2%	Folate	2%
Vitamin B₁₂	8%	Biotin	1%
Pantothenate	0%	Phosphorus	12%
Iodine	1%	Magnesium	4%
Zinc	5%	Selenium	9%
Copper	1%	Manganese	2%
Chromium	1%	Molybenum	1%
Chloride	1%		

* Percent Daily Values are based on a 2,000 Calorie diet. Your daily values may be higher or lower depending on your Calorie needs.

		Calories: 2,000	2,500
Total Fat	Less than	65 g	80 g
Saturated + Trans	Less than	20 g	25 g
Cholesterol	Less than	300 mg	300 mg
Sodium	Less than	2,400 mg	2,400 mg
Potassium		3,500 mg	3,500 mg
Total Carbohydrate		300 g	375 g
Dietary Fibre		25 g	30 g

Calories per gram:
Fat 9   Carbohydrate 4   Protein 4

Yogurt: A

Nutrition Facts
Serving Size 100g
Servings Per Container 1

Amount Per Serving

Calories 94   Calories from Fat 2

	% Daily Value*
Total Fat 0g	0 %
Saturated 0g	1 %
+ Trans Fat 0g	
Cholesterol 2mg	1 %
Sodium 58mg	2 %
Total Carbohydrate 19g	6 %
Dietary Fibre 0g	0 %
Sugars 19g	
Protein 4 g	

Vitamin A	0 %	Vitamin C	1 %
Calcium	15 %	Iron	0 %

* Percent Daily Values are based on a 2,000 calorie diet. Your Daily Values may be higher or lower depending on your Calorie needs.

		Calories: 2,000	2,500
Total Fat	Less than	65 g	80 g
Sat Fat	Less than	20 g	25 g
Cholesterol	Less than	300 mg	300 mg
Sodium	Less than	2,400 mg	2,400 mg
Total Carbohydrate		300 g	375 g
Dietary Fibre		25 g	30 g

Calories per gram:
Fat 9   Carbohydrate 4   Protein 4

Yogurt: A

Nutrition Facts
Per 100 g

Amount	% Daily Value
Energy 94 kcal	
Fat 0 g	0%
Saturated 0 g	1%
+ Trans 0 g	
Cholesterol 2 mg	1%
Sodium 58 mg	2%
Carbohydrate 19 g	6%
Fibre 0 g	0%
Sugars 19 g	
Protein 4 g	

Vitamin A 0 IU	0%	Vitamin C 6 mg	1%
Calcium 20 mg	15%	Iron 4.5 mg	0%

Short Canadian   **Short American**   **Long American**

CHAPTER 2

What's Organic? The Politics and Policy of the Practice and Label in the 21st Century

Samantha L. Mosier (East Carolina University)

Organic is a hallmark of the alternative and sustainable food system. Once a fringe market and production system, organic food and agriculture is now a multi-billion dollar industry—globally, and the United States is the single largest market. In 2017, organic sales in the U.S. reached $49.4 billion with 2018 indicators suggesting a significant spike in market activity due to Millennial and Hispanic household purchases (Nielsen, 2018; OTA, 2018). The growth in the market comes after several decades of legitimization efforts driven by organic farming advocates seeking to regulate the market, initially through third-party certification options and then eventual government regulations. Organic farming and food, as we know it today, emerged during the 20th century in response to new industrial technologies and practices that began changing the agricultural landscape and foodscapes. Organic farming was a method and lifestyle that sought to address the woes of declining soil quality, maintain or improve dietary needs, and engage with deeper philosophical concerns about farming and the environment. Along the way, organic has become more narrowly defined, a byproduct of being one of the oldest and most highly regulated terms in the alternative agriculture market.

Governments began regulating organic farming and labeling in the 1970s after several decades of third-party organizations, such as the Rodale Institute, initiating and implementing voluntary farming standards alongside educational programming. U.S. states, such as Oregon and California, were the first governmental entities to regulate what food products could be labeled as organic. Twenty-eight additional states would follow in the footsteps of Oregon and California before Congress adopted the Organic Food Production Act (OFPA) in 1990. The bill was an effort to eliminate the patchwork of emerging state-level standards in light of international norms that could create additional trade pressures. However, the bill would not officially go into effect until 2002 because of a number of delays in approving the NOP final rule. Unfortunately, even with government intervention in the market, there still remains some confusion and outright hostile debates about what organic actually means. Organic, similar to other eco-label terms such as natural or local, is rife with misinformation among consumers and even producers. For others, the term has been greenwashed and succumbed to corporate influence. As such, to discuss the challenges with the organic market is to consider the historical events, political debates, and philosophical ideas that underlie the practice. In what follows, a brief history on organic food policy is provided before delving into specific contemporary debates about organic practices and advertising since the National Organic Program (NOP) was finalized in 2002. One key and perpetual challenge is compromising the battle of multiple perspectives on what it means to be organic into a singular and unified definition and standard. This has been a problem since the formation of the practice and market itself. Through regulation, the battle to define organic has led to winners and losers with both consumers and producers facing difficult decisions as a new beyond organic movement emerges.

A BRIEF HISTORY OF ORGANIC FOOD, AGRICULTURE, AND POLICY

It is not unusual to enter your local supermarket or grocery store today and see a wide variety of organic products available. Organic has become a common label and marketing strategy to promote foods that have met the requirements of the USDA National Organic Program (NOP). However, the organic label is truly a 21st century phenomenon. If you were to search for organic products in the twentieth century, you would likely not find any such items available at your local grocery store. Organic foods, whether certified or not, were part of the fringe alternative market often available to consumers through farmers markets, food co-ops, and natural grocers starting in the mid twentieth century. To be an organic farmer and consumer was to operate within a market that was not supported by the mainstream and was perceived at odds with the norms of modern agricultural production and consumption patterns. Organic only became a mainstream practice after several decades of legitimizing the practice under organic advocacy groups and the eventual government regulation of the market by law.

To understand the policy debates, one must also understand the history and philosophy behind the term "organic.' Agriculture became highly mechanized and dependent on a range of new agricultural technologies to increase efficiency and improve overall yields during the twentieth century. Conventional or industrial agriculture boomed in the post-WWII environment. Mechanization, off-farm inputs (e.g. synthetic fertilizers and pesticides), monocropping, and biotechnology are hallmarks of industrial agriculture that still exist today. Organic farming emerged in response to industrialized agriculture, which is perceived as disconnected from the natural world. Undeniably, there are many consequences that result from industrialized practices including soil and environmental degradation, rising inequalities, risks to human health, and the decline of the family farm (Norberg-Hodge, Goerin, and Page 1993; Lobao and Meyer 2001). Organic farming, conversely, seeks to maintain an intimate connection to the natural and holistic while directly rejecting the unnatural (Niggli, 2007; Stinner, 2007). Early proponents of organic farming, such as Eve Balfour, Albert Howard, and Rudolph Steiner, each advocated a slightly different approach to organic farming but upheld a general standard of holistic farm management that upheld the values of health, ecology, fairness, and caring (O'Sullivan, 2015; Sligh and Cierpka, 2007; Stinner,

2007; Vogt, 2007). The values crafted an image of a sustainable practice that created a healthy environment and ethically sound form of agricultural production.

The first push to legitimize and protect the term and practice came with the emergence of organic agriculture groups and certification. The Rodale Institute, founded in 1947 as the Soil and Health Foundation, is one of the foremost organic associations that provided education, support, and self-regulation to the practice. By the 1970s, Rodale expanded research efforts through the acquisition of 333-acre Pennsylvania farm and also managed to create an organic certification program for organic farmers through Rodale Press' *Organic Gardening and Farming Magazine* (CCOF 1988; Rodale Institute ND). The California Organic Farmers Association, now known as California Certified Organic Farmers (CCOF), and Regional Tilth, better known today as Oregon Tilth, also provided support for organic farmers in the western United States, and each organization established their own organic certification programs in 1973 and 1982, respectively. Remarkably, each certification program was grounded in similar standards with only minimal variation in practices. The sudden emergence of certification programs among organic agriculture associations is not by chance. The intentional move to create some sort of accountability mechanism was a defensive move. The organic and natural food market was a profitable endeavor and one that was susceptible to scams and fraudulent advertising. The creation of a grower-focused industry checkpoint provided some solace to consumers seeking truth-in-labeling and boosted confidence in a burgeoning market.

If grower association certification programs were a defensive move, the offensive move for organic advocates was to pursue government regulations, which began in the 1970s. Oregon became the first state to adopt formal regulations regarding the production and sale of organic-labeled foods in 1973. California, Connecticut, Main, and New York would follow later in the decade (Mosier, 2017; Mosier and Thilmany, 2016). Organic advocacy groups were often behind the helms of early government efforts to regulate. The laws adopted are reflective of the uneasy relationship between organic farmers and government regulators, the latter which often favored industrial interests in policy. This relationship continues to be uneasy to this day. The rush to regulate the market really took off in the late 1980s as organic associations began to mature and professionalize, organic foods became mainstream, and fraud continued as a major concern. By the end of 1990, the same year Congress adopted the Organic Food Production Act (OFPA) as Title XXI of the 1990 Farm Bill, 29 states had adopted their own policies for organic regulatory standards either through state legislation or administrative rules. The rapid diffusion in the 1980s came in the midst of elevated attention, both positive and negative, to organic foods through such events as the Alar scare and California carrot caper scandal.[1] State governments sought to fill a need to strictly regulate the market left

---

[1] The carrot caper scandal occurred in 1988 after photos surfaced of Pacific Organics, a food distributor in southern California, rebagging conventionally grown carrots into organic packaging. This scandal was a major case of fraud that rocked the organic community. The Alar scare occurred a year later in 1989 after a *60 Minutes* segment featuring Meryl Streep highlighted the dangers of pesticides, including Alar. The focusing event drastically increased demand for organic produce (Mosier, 2017).

void by the federal government's lack of regulatory intervention. Indeed, the Federal Trade Commission considered but ultimately passed on creating organic standards and defining natural foods in the late 1970s (Mosier, 2017). As such, the rush to regulate by state governments was an effort to bring more stringent oversight on market activities.

Adoption of the OFPA was a victory for many. Congressional efforts took nearly two years before the passage of national law. However, the OFPA would not fully materialize until 2002, when the National Organic Program Final Rule went into effect. In the twelve years that passed, some states continued to adopt their own rules, unsure if the national law would materialize. Moreover, the twelve year delay highlighted the changing nature of the organic market and the subtle rifts between various sects of organic farmers. The market was rapidly growing with an uptick in corporate interests. The long-held concerns over the corporate influence on organic production became obvious during the 1997 NOP proposed rule period. Nearly 250,000 comments were received by the end of open comment period, most critical of the proposed rule.[2] If the standards proposed went into effect, organic would lose credibility as an alternative to industrial. The three biggest criticisms centered on the permissible used of irradiation, sewage sludge, and genetically engineered organisms in production (Rawson, 1998). The final rule ultimately would not allow the three controversial practices, but the reputation and capability of the National Organic Standards Board (NOSB) and the NOP was damaged. State governments would continue to pursue their own regulations until the announcement of the final rule was published in December 2001, much like the time period where the national law floundered in mid-1990s (Mosier, 2017). Furthermore, the program would face litigation immediately after the NOP final rule went into effect with the plaintiff claiming the standards still did not adhere to the OFPA purpose. The courts sided with the plaintiff on three counts, which forced the program standards to be adjusted (Viña, 2006). The delayed and controversial beginning of the NOP highlights the challenges associated with the organic label in the largest global organic market.

SOME CONTEMPORARY CHALLENGES IN REGULATION

The NOP has persisted in its efforts to oversee the organic market and update standards to reflect changing conditions to represent a wider scope of certified products (e.g. dairy, meats, textiles, aquaculture, pet food, etc.) and changing methods of production (e.g. hydroponic, use of synthetic inputs, etc.). There are a few key and visible issues that demonstrate the depths of the contemporary organic market, and challenges for interpreting the label including livestock and poultry rules, aquaculture, and hydroponics. Collectively, each issue highlights underlying differences for how the organic label should be used amongst increasingly skeptical and misinformed consumers and organic advocates displeased with corporatization

---

[2] Some accounts report figures higher and lower that 250,000. Possible reasons include duplicate submissions, multiple submissions by a singular individual or organization, or other challenges associated with collecting comments during the administrative rule process.

of the market. To many organic advocates, the regulations developed for the expanding market are dismissive to key tenants of production, namely a commitment to improving soil and general welfare, that derive from the historical norms and philosophical spirit of the practice. As highlighted in the examples below, the expanding market is challenged with variation in sectors and products seeking the organic seal while maintaining the original intent of the movement.

Livestock and Poultry

Livestock and poultry rules have been an ongoing and complicated issue for the NOP. Key tenants of debate for livestock and poultry center on origin, feed, and welfare. Similar to land conversion wait periods for organic crops, livestock and poultry are also bound to expectations for conversion into production and overall treatment. For example, it is expected that organic livestock used in dairy production must be subjected to organic management practices from the last third of gestation or thatching (7 CFR 205.236) and, in terms of welfare and feed, have adequate access to pasture or organic feed during periods of confinement (7 CFR 205.237 - 205.239). Unfortunately, there remain loopholes in the law that mostly benefit larger producers, such as origin rules,[3] and continue to permit questionable modifications to livestock and poultry such as tail docking, tusk removal, and debeaking, which is considered inhumane and unethical to many organic advocates. As part of the general philosophical intentions of organic agriculture, animal welfare is a central tenant to the practice, and ensuring that all producers and distributors adhere to sound organic handling practices is key to maintaining the sector's reputation.

Rules were developed during President Obama's administration to address some of the shortcomings of organic regulations for livestock and poultry. The Organic Livestock and Poultry Practices (OLPP) final rule was published on January 19, 2017 as the cumulative result. The rule would resolve the inconsistent practices for transitioning operations, provide fairness in production, and ultimately address concerns about ethical and humane treatment of livestock and poultry (National Organic Program, 2017). The final rule was the result of ten years of work by the industry and the USDA about overhauling standards to deal with issues of humane treatment of animals and to close some of the gaps in production practices. Notably, the origin of livestock issue has its own set of proposed rules for updating standards. However, the gains made through the OLPP rule would not materialize, as the final rule implementation was delayed three times before being withdrawn in December 2017 under pressure from President Trump's new administration. The OLPP received widespread support among the organic industry with only 50 of the 72,000 comments received about the rule withdrawal providing support for the

---

[3] Current organic standards require dairy cows to be continuously managed as organic from the last third of gestation. However, current regulations also permit dairy cows to be converted under a one-time rule due to a shortage in available stock in 1990. The latter rule permits conventional stock into organic operations without meeting the former rule. The NOSB has yet to adopt a proposed rule that would address the loophole despite pressure from industry advocates (National Organic Coalition, 2019.)

action (83 FR 10775). The almost immediate reaction by supporters was to file suit, highlighting an on-going rift of the many organic producers that "follow the spirit of the law" against large producers that simply seek to cash-in on the burgeoning market (Curry, 2017). The issue has yet to be resolved in court, and the origin of livestock final rule is still not published.

Aquaculture

Aquaculture also has an extensive history within the NOP and has generated its own sets of controversy. Currently, the NOP has not developed standards for aquaculture but has been under consideration by the program since its inception. Indeed, an aquatic animals task force was announced in 2005 with a final report with recommendations for aquaculture published in October 2010 (Aquaculture Working Group, 2010). No action, however, has been made on the final set of recommendations and technical questions still remain regarding contribution to soil health and the use and exposure to synthetic materials in production (Hopkin, 2013). Instead, other countries and third-party organizations have developed standards that generally guide activity in the U.S. market, but they have varying requirements and standards.[4] Developing guidelines for aquaculture is difficult given it is not a production sector that can adequately connect to soil stewardship, an issue that also plagues hydroponics (Gould, Compagnoni, and Lembo, 2019). Aquaculture production instead relies on either production in natural bodies of water, leading to potential contamination of non-organic approved substances, or synthetic and confined environments, which goes against principles of humane and ethical behavior (Burden, 2009; Hopkinson, 2013). Aquaculture's struggle for the USDA organic seal will rest on the sector's ability to connect to other tenants of the organic spirit including health, ecology, fairness, and care; this will balance the needs of producers while maintaining the sanctity of the term for consumers (Gould, Compagnoni, and Lembo, 2019).

Hydroponics, Aquaponics, and Aeroponics

Produce from hydroponic, aquaponic, and aeroponic operations are officially able to carry the organic seal after a close 8-7 vote by the NOSB in 2017. The NOP clearly provides acceptance of hydroponic products as organic. Hydroponic production has been an issue of concern by the NOP since the program's inception, similar to livestock and poultry rules. In 2010, the NOSB stood behind a subcommittee report and recommendation to not permit hydroponic operations to be certified organic. The premise was largely grounded in the production system lacking contribution to improving soil quality and health. The subcommittee held the belief that soil fertility is a central tenant to organic production and hydroponic production is unable to address that concern. This issue was considered again by the Hydroponic

---

[4] Chase, Alexandra. 2016. Organic Aquaculture Standards: Navigating Potential USDA Regulations. Webinar, National Agricultural Law Center, April 20. Accessed at https://nationalaglawcenter.org/consortium/webinars/organicaquaculture/

and Aquaponic Task Force in 2015 after no official rules were developed to ban hydroponic operations from becoming certified organic. The task force recommended the NOSB to develop official rules to regulate organic hydroponic operations, which the committee called bioponics to distinguish the practice from conventional hydroponic operations (Hydroponic and Aquaponic Task Force, 2016). The 2017 vote officially permitted certification of hydroponic, or rather bioponic, operations.

The response to the 2017 NOSB vote has not been positive. The organic community remains divided with a particular sect being unwelcoming to bioponic growers both for philosophical and economic reasons (Perkowski, 2017). In fact, the Center for Food Safety filed a rulemaking petition in 2019 for the USDA to prohibit organic hydroponic operations, which received support from a number of other organic groups including the Cornucopia Institute and Organic Farmers Association. The center cited failure of hydroponics to comply with organic soil requirements, undercutting traditional organic farming operations, and degrading consumer trust in the organic label (Center for Food Safety, 2019). To date, the USDA has not responded officially to the petition but has acknowledged some administrative challenges for certifying operations (Karst, 2019).

DEFINING ORGANIC: THE MALLEABILITY OF MEANING IN AN ERA OF MISINFORMATION

The organic market and USDA program have matured since the 1990 Farm Bill. The challenges the term and label face today are, at the core, based on the nature of using a singular term to cover inherently complex processes and value systems. The NOP does provide very specific standards and guidelines, but the term "organic" has been historically flexible across various sects and is intertwined with other alternative systems rebelling against an industrial system. As O'Sullivan (2015) states, "...the term "organic' has often been malleable enough to be pulled and twisted by rival factions, leaving a trail of misconceptions. Its elements [are] ideologically charged." Undeniably, organic is and will continue to be an umbrella term despite governments best intentions to provide a singularly defined concept in practice. Indeed, the NOP push to provide a singular definition is what has driven many to criticize government policies as too accommodating, particularly of large-scale and industrial interests, while failing to truly protect smaller operators that were at the core of the movement and initiation for regulations. As such, the legacy of a plastic term leads to challenges as the industry and market mature.

Those within the industry and some scholars have described the differences and debates within the organic market as those of a consumer versus producer perspective on organic (Clark 2015; Haedicke 2016; Mosier, 2017; Obach 2015). The consumer perspective is a more stringent approach that is embodied in the current national standards. Originating from such state regulations like those adopted in California, the consumer perspective strives to create a singular definition that is largely driven by consumer needs and seeks to eliminate misinformation by providing a uniform standard. Conversely, the producer perspective, most notably observed in state regulations like those in Vermont, is driven by the needs of producers with standards permitting more flexibility in defining and adhering to organic principles. More attention is allotted to producers, who should take center stage for determining standards, and the standards essentially eliminate or severely limit the input of large corporate interests and inexperienced administrators. Unlike the consumer perspective, the producer perspective is not concerned with under- or misinformed consumers and, by extension, producers. Instead, the focus is on expert and experienced producers driving regulatory norms, which could permit a base minimum for being organic with leeway to engage in more intensive practices.

The division between consumer and producer perspectives may be a bit simplified. In truth the divide, and therefore the basis for malleability of the term, is partially grounded in misinformation and misunderstanding of agricultural production and food labels. It could be an understatement to suggest that misinformation and ignorance is present in the market. In reality, it is rampant. Consumers demonstrate support for organic food and agriculture, evident by increasing sales, but there are numerous reports and studies that indicate lack of knowledge and awareness about what consumers are actually supporting (for example see Schleenbeck and Hamm, 2013; Sikavica and Pozner, 2013). The organic label is often confused for or equated to other labels including local, natural, non-GMO, and ethically and humanely raised. Historically, natural foods have been the most competitive and closely aligned to the organic label, as evident by Federal Trade Commission investigations in the late 1970s. In addition to label confusion, a number of consumers also believe that organic foods are produced by small-scale farms and are free from pesticides and fertilizers, which is not factually correct. Consumers are drawn to the organic for a variety of reasons including health, environment, welfare, and general pleasure of food (Bonti-Ankomag and Yiridoe, 2006; Hughner et. al., 2007). Many of these same reasons also drive consumers into other sects of the alternative food market thereby contributing to overall confusion for what one term and production method means versus another.

The level of confusion the organic label and alternative market faces is not in solitude. In general, consumers demonstrate a lack of knowledge and general confusion about the food system as a whole. For example, the Michigan State University Food Literacy and Engagement Poll in 2017 demonstrated that 66% of American-based respondents were highly influenced by food labels with approximately 37% of surveyed population also believing that non-GMO foods did not contain genes or DNA. Confounding the findings is that 42% of responds believed they have an average understanding of the global food system while 37% reported an above average knowledge. In general, it seems that the general public believes itself to be knowledgeable about the food system but collectively fails to admit shortcomings in knowledge and susceptibility to labeling when making decisions. The Michigan State University study is not alone in its findings. Other studies highlight serious problems with consumer knowledge and ability to make informed decisions particularly within the alternative or sustainable food market (Abrams et al. 2009; Burton 2004; Gutierrez and Thornton 2014; Gwira Baumblatt et al. 2017; McFadden and Lusk 2016; National Academies of Sciences, Engineering, and Medicine 2016; Rumble et al. 2014).

Producers also share some of the blame when it comes to misinformation. Some of the misinformation generated by producers is truly unintentional. For example, producers selling in farmers' markets may sell "organic' produce but not fully follow the law, perhaps ignorant or unaware of the necessary processes to be organic compliant.[5] Some misinformation has also been intentional misguidance and outright fraud. Historical cases like the California Carrot Caper highlight fraud in the marketplace (Guthman, 2004; Mosier, 2016). Yet, misinformation from producers also derives from marketing strategies selling a particular image that is not completely true, crossing elements of both intentional and unintentional misinformation. Organic can be sold on the imagining of purity and the uncorrupted (Interview with Organic Farmer and Policy Expert, October 28, 2016). This image can generate sales among consumers looking for food purity in a perceived world of contamination caused by industrial practices. However, the organic food market is now dominated by large corporate interests. An organic operation could be certified with the resultant products carrying the USDA organic seal, but the product itself is likely a product owned and sold by one of a handful of international conglomerates (Howard, 2016). The image of small-farm, local, and generally anti-establishment, which are also the some of the same premises in which natural foods are often sold (Sagoff, 2001), is incorrect. Organic is big business and the choir of organic advocates may be quite correct to claim corporate co-option of the market and too heavy of involvement and domination in the regulatory process.

The rise of corporate involvement in the market was predicted by some as an inevitable result of adopting a federal law based on a consumer perspective (Mosier, 2016). Minimizing the voices of producers and failing to permit variation in organic operations opened the ability for larger producers to overtake the market to meet rising demand and prevent more stringent regulatory rules beneficial to more intensive operations. It would be incorrect to suggest that the current set of organic regulatory rules completely eliminated all consumer trust in the market or completely eliminated adherence to an organic ethos among currently certified producers (Carter et. al., 2019). However, the organic label is struggling as many consumers and producers question the legitimacy of the program amidst controversial decisions that economically benefit larger interests while degrading the original spirit of the law. Misinformation and confusion undermine the label and market potential. As such, a new era of organics has emerged to encourage a return to the original intention of the movement.

KEEPING IT REAL: BEYOND ORGANIC AND THE REGENERATIVE MOVEMENT

Admittedly, the organic consumers and producers of today are quite different than those thirty to forty years ago. Diversification and mainstreaming of the market

---

[5]Alexandria Chase, "Organic Aquaculture Standards: Navigating Potential USDA Regulations," webinar April 20, 2016, National Agricultural Law Center, https://nationalaglawcenter.org/consortium/webinars/organicaquaculture/.

have led to a range of consumers and producers with some more knowledgeable about organic practices than others, and clear variations in commitment to core organic principles. As such, those consumers and producers dedicated to more stringent organic regulations have established their own beyond organic certification programs. The Real Organic Project and Regenerative Organic Alliance now offer certification and support for producers and businesses that are already certified organic under the NOP and seek to demonstrate a deeper commitment to the organic ethos. Both programs cite failures of the USDA to regulate the organic market appropriately, attacking both hydroponic operations and livestock rulings.

The Real Organic Project (ROP) was announced in 2018 after a series of meetings among Vermont farmers. In an open letter, the ROP (2018) states, "For the many people who have spent years working hard to build the integrity of the NOP, this is a dismal moment. We have lost the helm, and the New Organic will not have much to do with the ideals of such pioneers as Albert Howard and Eve Balfour. It will have to do with money. Money will decide what is called "certified organic' and what isn't." This is a similar reason for the emergence of the Regenerative Organic Certified (ROC) program. Regenerative Organic Alliance (ROA) is led by the Rodale Institute, Patagonia, and Dr. Bronner's with the ROC serving as the Alliance's certification program. ROC is built upon three pillars—soil health, animal welfare, and social fairness—that go beyond sustainability (ROA, 2019). The framework of the program was announced in 2017 with pilot program audits completed in the summer of 2019.

ROP and the ROA are the next frontier for the organic label. The producer-oriented programs are clear critiques on the consumer-driven NOP standards and guidelines. The emergence of beyond organic is perhaps not surprising. A malleable term needs flexibility in regulatory achievement, particularly in a market where the diversity of products and producers is high. The first products certified by the ROP and ROA will enter the markets starting in late 2019.

THE FUTURE OF ORGANIC

Organic is a highly regulated term and a concept that has become embattled in controversy. The struggle to define organic has not been easy. Early advocates for organic farming and food struggled to define and protect the term and concept from corporate interests that already were greenwashing and manipulating the concept of natural foods. Certifying organic operations and seeking government policies that would protect the sanctity of meaning were important to protect market activity. However, it appears the adoption of a more restrictively singular definition or consumer-based approach to regulating the market has undermined the ability of the NOP to contend with the malleability of organic. The regulatory design has led to significant political and corporate influence leading to a decline in trust as well as truth in labeling.

It should not be forgotten that organic has never been a singular production method. It represents a variety of production methods encompassed within a community. The ties that bind this community together are grounded in a particular ethos of philosophy, science, and anti-corporatization. The failure of the NOP to contend with variation in organic production has led us all into a new era of beyond organic. Consumers and producers in the market will now contend with yet another set of labels. The USDA organic seal and the NOP will likely continue to flourish, but there will be additional challenges to the market as beyond organic alternatives emerge. It is likely that additional beyond organic labels will continue to confuse consumers or at least a segment of consumers that are not well educated or versed in the roots of organic farming.

For those consumers and producers truly seeking holistic organic ethos, the beyond organic labels offer an outlet to provide the extra assurance of quality. It is unlikely that the beyond organic groups will be co-opted by large corporate interests or new organic market segments beyond what may have already occurred. Both the ROP and ROA were created and founded by more producer-oriented organic interest groups seeking to eliminate the tarnishing effect of singular approach to organic that could cover every market segment. While it is impossible to predict the future, the beyond organic movement at least bolsters the organic market as a whole while simultaneously adding an additional layer of competitiveness for products grown and sold as "organic ".

REFERENCES

Abrams, Katie M., Courtney A. Meyers, and Tracy A. Irani. "Naturally Confused: Consumers' Perceptions of All-natural and Organic Pork Products." *Agriculture and Human Values*, 27, no.3 (2009): 365-74.

Aquaculture Working Group. 2010. "Report with Final Recommendations 10-11-10." United States Department of Agriculture National Organic Programs. Accessed at https://www.ams.usda.gov/rules-regulations/organic/nosb/task-forces

Bonti-Ankomah, Samuel, Emmanuel K. Yiridoe. "Organic and Conventional Food: A Literature Review of the Economics of Consumer Perceptions and Preferences." *Organic Agriculture Centre of Canada*, 59 (2006): 1-40.

Burden, Dan. "The Organic Aquaculture Quandary." *Agricultural Marketing Resource Center*. Accessed at https://www.agmrc.org/commodities-products/aquaculture/the-organic-aquaculture-quandary

Burton, Scot and Elizabeth H. Creyer. "What Consumers Don't Know *Can* Hurt Them: Consumer Evaluations and Disease Risk Perceptions of Restaurant Menu Items." *Journal of Consumer Affairs*, 38, no.1 (2004): 121-145.

California Certified Organic Farmers [CCOF]. "Our Story So Far: CCOF Marks 15th Anniversary." *California Certified Organic Farmers Statewide Newsletter*, 5 no.2 (1988): 1-3.

Carter, David, Samantha L. Mosier, and Ian Adams. "How Values Shape Program Perceptions: The "Organic Ethos' and Producers' Perceptions of U.S. Organic Policy Impacts." *Review of Policy Research*, 36, no.3 (2019): 296-317.

Center for Food Safety. 2019. "Center for Food Safety Files Legal Action to Prohibit Hydroponics from Organic." Accessed at https://www.centerforfoodsafety.org/press-releases/5501/center-for-food-safety-files-legal-action-to-prohibit-hydroponics-from-organic

Clark, Lisa F. The Changing Politics of Organic Food in North America. Northampton, MA: Edward Elgar (2015).

Curry, Lynne. 2017. "Years in the Making, Organic Animal Welfare Rules Killed by Trump's USDA." Civil Eats. Accessed at https://civileats.com/2017/12/18/years-in-the-making-trumps-usda-kills-organic-animal-welfare-rules/

Gould, David, Antonio Compagnoni, and Giuseppe Lembo. "Organic Aquaculture: Principles, Standards and Certification." In *Organic Aquaculture: Impacts and Future Developments*. Switzerland; Springer (2019).

Guthamn, Julie. *Agrarian Dreams: The Paradox of Organic Farming in California*. Berkeley, California: University of California Press (2004).

Gutierrez, Alexis and Thomas Thornton. 2014. "Can Consumers Understand Sustainability through Seafood Eco-Labels? A U.S. and UK Case Study." *Sustainability*, 6, no.1 (2014): 8195-8217.

Gwira Baumblatt, Jane A., L.Rand Carpenter, Caleb Wiederman, John R. Dunn, William Schaffner, and Timothy F. Jones. "Population Survey of Attitudes and Beliefs Regarding Organic, Genetically Modified, and Irradiated Foods." *Nutrition and Health*, 23, no.1 (2017):7-11.

Haedicke, Michael A. *Organizing Organic*. Stanford University Press (2016).

Hopkinson, Jenny. 2013. "Rules for Farm Fish Come Slowly." *Politico.* Accessed at https://www.politico.com/story/2013/10/organic-standards-for-aquaculture-are-slow-moving-099057

Howard, Philip H. Concentration and Power in the Food System: Who Controls What We Eat? London: Bloomsbury Academic (2016).

Hughner, Renée Shaw, Pierre McDonagh, Andrea Prothero, Clifford J. Schultz II, and Julie Stanton. "Who Are Organic Food Consumers? A Compilation and Review of Why People Purchase Organic Food." *Journal of Consumer Behaviour: An International Research Review*, 6, no.2-3 (2007): 94-110.

Hydroponic and Aquaponic Task Force. 2016. *Hydroponic and Aquaponic Task Force Report*. National Organic Standards Board, United State Department of Agriculture Agricultural Marketing Service National Organic Program. Accessed at https://www.ams.usda.gov/sites/default/files/media/2016%20Hydroponic%20Task%20Force%20Report.PDF

Karst, Tom. 2019. "Tucker: Hydroponic Certification is Settled Issue." The Packer. Accessed at https://www.thepacker.com/article/tucker-hydroponic-organic-certification-settled-issue

Lobao, Linda, and Katherine Meyer. "The Great Agricultural Transition: Crisis, Change, and Social Consequences of Twentieth-Century U.S. Farming." *Annual Review of Sociology*, 27 (2001): 103-24.

McFadden, Brandon R. and Jayson L. Lusk. "What Consumers Don't Know about Genetically Modified Food, and How that Affects Beliefs." *The FASEB Journal*, 30, no.9 (2016): 3091-3096.

Michigan State University Food Literacy and Engagement Poll. 2017. "MSU Food Literacy and Engagement Poll." Accessed at http://www.canr.msu.edu/news/msu-food-literacy-and-engagement-poll

Mosier, Samantha L. Creating Organic Standards in U.S. States: The Diffusion of State Organic Food and Agriculture Legislation. Lexington Books (2017).

Mosier, Samantha L., and Dawn Thilmany. "Diffusion of Food Policy in the U.S.: The Case of Organic Certification." *Food Policy*, 61 (2016): 80-91.

National Academies of Sciences, Engineering, and Medicine. *Genetically Engineered Crops: Experiences and Prospects*. Washington, D.C. (2016).

National Organic Coalition. 2019. "Organic Enforcement & Fraud." Accessed at https://www.nationalorganiccoalition.org/organic-enforcement-and-fraud

National Organic Program. 2017. "Organic Livestock and Poultry Practices Final Rule: Questions and Answers – January 2017." USDA Agricultural Marketing Service. Accessed at https://www.ams.usda.gov/sites/default/files/media/OLPPExternalQA.pdf

Nielsen. 2018. "Tops of 2018: Organic." Nielsen Insights. Accessed at https://www.nielsen.com/us/en/insights/news/2018/tops-of-2018-organic.html

Norberg-Hodge, Helena, Peter Goering, and John Page. *From the Ground Up: Rethinking Industrial Agriculture*. London: Zed Books (1993).

Obach, Brian K. Organic Struggle: The Movement for Sustainable Agriculture in the United States. Cambridge, MA: MIT Press (2015).

O'Sullivan, Robin. American Organic: A Cultural History of Farming, Gardening, Shopping, and Eating. Lawrence, KS: University Press of Kansas (2015).

Organic Trade Association [OTA]. 2018. "U.S. Organic Industry Survey 2018." Access available at https://ota.com/resources/organic-industry-survey

Perkowski, Mateusz. 2017. Organic Hydoponics Likely to Provoke Legal Challenge. *Capital Press.* Accessed at https://www.capitalpress.com/nation_world/ap_nation_world/organic-hydroponics-likely-to-provoke-legal-challenge/article_2776fb92-f7f2-59b2-8da0-b85529c9f912.html

Rawson, Jean M. Congressional Research Service. 1998. *Organic Foods and the Proposed Federal Certification and Labeling Program.* Accessed at http://crs.ncseonline.org/NLE/CRSreports/Agriculture/ag-54.cfm#4

Real Organic Project (ROP). 2018. "Real Organic Project is Being Born." *Medium*. Accessed at https://medium.com/@realorganicproj/realorganiclaunch-c31e274012b6

Regenerative Organic Alliance (ROA). 2019. "About." Accessed at https://regenorganic.org

Rodale Institute. 2019. "Our Story." Accessed on July 1, 2019 at https://rodaleinstitute.org/about/our-story/

Rumble, Joy N., Jessica Holt, and Tracy Irani. "The Power of Words: Exploring Consumers' Perceptions of Words Commonly Associated with Agriculture." *Journal of Applied Communications*, 98, no.2 (2014): Art. 3.

Schleenbecker, Rosa, and Ulrich Hamm. "Consumers' Perception of Organic Product Characteristics. A Review." *Appetite*, 71, no.1 (2013): 420-429.

Sikavica, Katarina, and Jo-Ellen Pozner. "Paradise Sold: Resource Partitioning and the Organic Movement in the US Farming Industry." *Organization Studies*, 34 no.5-6 (2013): 623-651.

Sligh, Michael, and Thomas Cierpka. "Organic Values." In *Organic Farming: An International History*, ed. William Lockeretz. Cambridge: CABI International (2007).

Viña, Stephen R. 2006. *Harvey v. Veneman* and the National Organic Program. CRS Report for Congress. Accessed at https://nationalaglawcenter.org/wp-content/uploads/assets/crs/RS22318.pdf

Vogt, Gunter. "The Origins of Organic Farming." In *Organic Farming: An International History*, ed. William Lockeretz. Cambridge: CABI International (2007).

CHAPTER 3

The Competitive Politics of Labeling Genetically Modified Foods, Now Bioengineered Foods

Gina L. Keel (State University of New York, Oneonta)

Labeling of genetically-modified foods has become a salient issue in many states, driven by the anti-GMO movement and pro-organic politics, and policy entrepreneurship. Across decision-making venues, two distinct advocacy coalitions with environmental and industry orientations struggled over genetically-modified (GM) food labeling. The history of their competitive venue shopping reflects policy wins and losses for each side. Institutional dimensions provide legal and political constraints to policy making, as well as opportunities for interest group advocacy and venue shifting. The U.S. political system is characterized by openness for interest group participation. Federalism with national supremacy, checks and balances among branches, and public rulemaking procedures carve channels that interest groups must navigate to influence policy making and regulation. These channels also provide opportunities to shift venues and extend policy conflict. Advocacy coalitions can lose in one forum and live to fight another day in another venue. The venues for GM food labeling battles have shifted among federal agencies, state legislatures, state ballot initiative drives, federal courts, and Congress.

Regulatory federalism empowers national laws and agency rules to preempt state actions. Yet, executive agencies can only draft rules within the authority granted by law, which provides openings for judicial review of agency actions. Federal regulators of foods, seeds, meats, and eggs are, primarily, the Food and Drug Administration and the United State Department of Agriculture. The biotechnology-agricultural industry has benefitted from promotional policies of both agencies and enjoyed discretion in labeling products, as long as their labels were truthful and not misleading. The FDA repeatedly cautioned against mandatory GM food labels and promoted appropriate voluntary labels. Congressional committees with jurisdictions in agriculture, commerce, and technology largely deferred to regulators and the established regime that had maximized producer and corporate freedoms on labeling. Labeling conflict escalated in the 1990s with local activism and state efforts to label milk from cows treated with genetically-engineered hormones designed to increase production. The Dairy industry successfully fought state legislation in federal courts, in two cases summarized below. The GMO labeling movement did not subside. Activists sought new state legislation and ballot initiatives to write laws that would survive judicial review. Vermont passed the nation's first mandatory GMO food labeling law in 2014, thereby triggering a venue shift back to federal courts and then national legislative venues.

Congress took up national GM labeling policy only after state initiatives threatened the status quo policy subsystem. In 2015 the food industry shifted their offensive strategy from federal courts to the Congress, which culminated in the summer of 2016 with the passage of a flexible "federal bioengineered food" disclosure law. Industry narratives dominated provisions in the new national policy on labeling, which preempted Vermont's mandatory genetically modified foods labeling law. The state's law requiring items be labeled "produced with genetic engineering" went into effect in July 1, 2016, after Congress' initial failure to pass end of session legislation due to mobilized opposition. A Senate compromise bill supported by President Obama achieved labeling preemption by August, and industry's federal lawsuit challenging Vermont was subsequently abandoned. The federal law also preempted Alaska's law requiring labels on genetically-modified salmon products sold in the state. The legislative outcome reconciled contradictory alternatives about how to label GM foods by requiring labeling in some form, such as QR (quick response) barcodes on packaging, but not requiring explicit label statements. Administrative rulemaking by USDA has been marked by delay and conflict, but the agency published a final rule for Bioengineered (BE) food disclosures in early 2019.

ADVOCACY COALITIONS

Grassroots groups with consumer, small farm, environmental health, and food safety orientations as well as organic food producers have advocated explicit mandatory GMO labeling, both in states and nationally. National advocacy groups involved in state and national venues include labeling-focused and anti-GMO organizations such as Center for Food Safety, Just Label It, Organic Consumers Association, Environmental Working Group, Food Democracy Now!, Food and Water Watch, Millions Against Monsanto, GMO Free USA, U.S. Right to Know, and Cornucopia Institute. Organic and natural food companies and grocers such as Stonyfield Organic, Nature's Path Organic, Annie's, National Cooperative Grocers, and Whole Foods Market are also part of the coalition. The Vermont Right to Know GMOs coalition led the state's movement and remains active; it includes Rural Vermont, Northeast Organic Farming Association of Vermont, Cedar Circle Farm, Vermont Public Interest Research Group, and a long list of supporting organizations and businesses such as Ben and Jerry's Ice Cream, 240 to 2019. The Truth in Labeling Coalition mobilized during the 2008 presidential campaign and secured commitments from Democratic candidates, including Barack Obama, to support national mandatory GMO labeling. But the labeling initiative was not a legislative priority post-election, compared to the economic crisis, healthcare reform, and climate policy. Democratic bills for mandatory labels became less likely when they lost control of the House. The labeling advocacy coalition won GMO label legislation in Connecticut (2013), Maine (2013), and Vermont (2014), and the movement seemed to be gaining ground in other states with labeling bills in 30 states during 2013-14. Maine and Connecticut passed laws that would not go into effect until neighboring states adopted similar laws, while Vermont passed a "no strings' attached law. At the signing, Vermont Governor Shumlin echoed the narrative of labeling advocates: "We believe we have a right to know what's in the food we buy" (CNN 2014). Alaska passed a GMO fish labeling law in 2005 to protect its fishing industry, anticipating USDA approval for genetically-engineered salmon that could be raised faster and fatter than conventional fish. The Center for Food Safety, National Organic Coalition, National Sustainable Agriculture Coalition, and Sierra Club were active in mobilizing public comments during the rulemaking process for the new BE disclosure law. The environmental agriculture and food coalition argued for clear, front of package labels meaningful to consumers and opposed digital disclosures as inaccessible and inequitable.

The industry advocacy coalition of pro-biotechnology agricultural science and giant food companies included Archer Daniels Midland, Campbell Soup, Coca-Cola, Dole, General Mills, Genetic Literacy Project, Kellogg, Mars, Monsanto, BASF, Bayer, Dow, and Syngenta. They allied in legislative and legal fights with grocery chains and were jointly represented by the Grocery Manufacturers Association (GMA), which claimed "more than 300 leading food, beverage, and consumer product companies." The food industry and its allies pushed the labeling issue into the national legislative venue, seeking preemptive legislation to serve their commercial interests. Large and small trade associations, business groups, and food and beverage companies were active in the rulemaking process for the new BE disclosure law, seeking to protect member interests, exclude feed and refined goods, and gain a flexible "marketing' standard. Associations submitting comments included GMA, American Farm Bureau, Chamber of Commerce, and National Association of Manufacturers, American Soybean Association, Beet Sugar Industry, International Dairy Foods Association, National Meat Institute, Food Marketing Institute, and Frozen Food Institute, among others.

The strategic narratives of the opposing coalitions shaped legislation in both houses of Congress during 2014-2016 and in subsequent USDA rulemaking is the focus of this chapter. The links between interest group and lawmaker narratives helps explain provisions of the final "bioengineered foods" disclosure legislation and bi-partisan support for preemption of state laws. The legislative intent created boundaries for USDA and the advocacy coalitions as they continued their struggles in BE disclosure rulemaking. The chapter concludes with examination of interest group narratives in rulemaking and their influence on the two BE label outcomes, along with a consideration of what's next in the ongoing policy conflict.

This case study follows policy change theory approaches by examining: 1) the strategic navigation of plural institutions and *venue shopping* by industry and environmental coalitions, and 2) groups' use of *competing narratives* about the problem and alternatives to advance their food system interests and values. Methods include narrative policy analysis of language and frames invoked by groups and repeated by lawmakers in congressional hearings and committee reports. In public documents, press releases, and interviews, lawmakers disclose their views of problem definitions, threats to favored constituencies, and policy solutions. Partisanship was not dominant in determining policy outcomes; rather, members from both parties found reasons to advance a national solution.

POLICY SUBSYSTEMS, VENUE SHOPPING, AND POLICY NARRATIVES

Policy change theorists seek to explain shifts in previously stable policy regimes. This case study relies upon advocacy coalition frameworks (Sabatier and Jenkins-Smith 1993) and narrative policy analysis (Stone 2012). These theories extend the pluralist approach in studying the roles of groups that either defend the status quo and policy monopolies, or promote policy change by attacking dominant groups' power and narratives. Policy change theories focusing on coalitions, venues, and narratives and these theories help illuminate the strategic use of plural institutions by industry and environmental groups to advance their food system interests and values. Quantitative approaches to narrative policy analysis (NPA) hypothesize and test group strategies. These scholars focus on comparing narrative strategies of "winners' that seek issue containment and status quo defense and "losers' that seek issue expansion and mobilization. Strategies include ways groups focus on winning and losing interests, who bears benefits and costs, how symbols are used to simplify, and how scientific authority is used to narrow debates (McBeth, Shanahan, Arnell, Hathaway 2007). Several of these group strategies are described in this case study with initial content analysis of frames, a preliminary step toward a quantitative approach.

Recent shifts in GM labeling policy can be understood through analyses of policy subsystem dynamics, including policy subsystem challenge and group competition through strategic venue choices and narratives. Policy subsystems, or issue-specific networks, are pervasive in American government because elected officials rely on the expertise of agency officials and interest groups in policymaking. Similarly, advocacy coalitions contain officials, interest group leaders, and researchers who share a belief system and show coordinated activity over time. Their beliefs about policy problems and solutions are reflected in narratives used to persuade or justify policy initiatives. "Cultural values, interest group advocacy, scientific information, and professional advice all help to shape the content of problem definition" and available policy alternatives (Rochefort and Cobb 1994). Advocacy coalitions compete to dominate policymaking in subsystems, and highly organized, resource-rich interest groups enjoy advantages. Subsystems are often characterized by routine policymaking with minor policy changes, but dominant coalitions can learn and adapt their "secondary" beliefs to new information about consequences of policy or challenges to their position in the subsystem (Sabatier and Jenkins-Smith 1993). Beliefs about appropriate policy tools and implementation are examples of adaption, and the food industry displayed an adaptive narrative strategy in GM labeling battles. They adapted to narrative and venue challenges from labeling advocates, and industry adapted as their interests evolved to favor labeling flexibility with a national standard determined by agency rulemaking. The USDA is now the venue for disputes over labeling rules.

Coalitions compete for policy influence and seek policy *defense* or policy *change* through agenda setting and issue framing. Problems can only get attention and policy action if framed in a compelling manner by advocacy coalitions comprised of groups and policymakers (Rochefort and Cobb 1994). Dominant groups try to maintain a privileged position by minimizing attention to alternate problem framing and policy solutions, while challenger groups call out to a broader audience, seek to expand debate, mobilize new participants and propose new policy actions. External pressures on dominant policy subsystems can upset the equilibrium and cause major, though infrequent, policy change and bursts of innovation (Baumgartner and Jones 1991). The GMO labeling advocates, with a popularly-supported "right to know what's in your food" narrative, challenged policy subsystems at state and national levels, and led to Vermont's expansive law; they also shaped the national labeling innovation.

In the U.S. federal system, policy conflict and competition occur in many decision venues, and interest groups can shape agendas and outcomes through *venue shopping* and strategic rhetoric in those venues (Morris 2007; Pralle 2009). Policy subsystem challenges may include venue shopping strategies to shift policy debate to a more promising venue. Groups challenge policy monopoly in one venue by seeking action in another. Venue and narrative strategies are dynamic; they shift when a coalition perceives it is losing. Losing groups try to redefine policy issues to increase general attention, mobilize supporters, and shift policy equilibrium (Baumgartner and Jones 1993; Stone 2012). Key venues are reflected below.

GMO Labeling Decision Venues

Policy shifts can be understood by analyzing subsystem dynamics and group competition through strategic venue choices and narratives. Mandatory GMO labeling advocates shifted the debate from resistant federal agencies to state legislatures and ballot initiatives. The industry coalition challenged state laws in federal courts, then switched to Congress to secure preemptive legislation. Groups now compete over Bio-engineering (BE) disclosure rules in USDA.

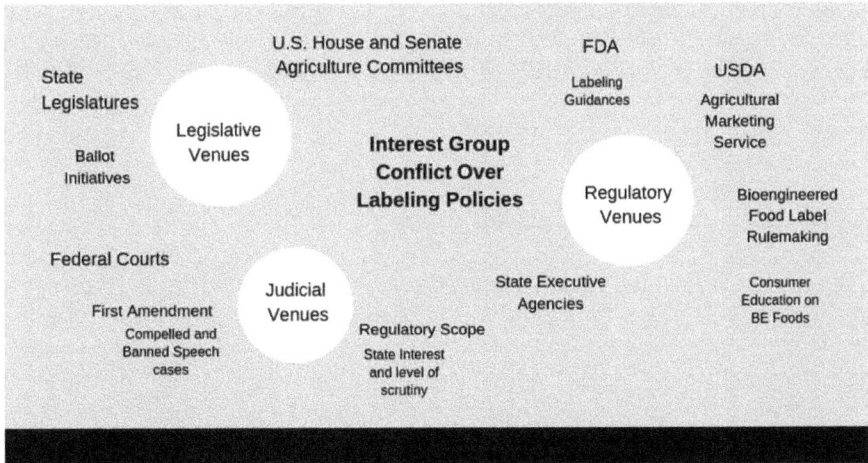

Labeling advocates shifted the labeling debate from resistant federal agencies to state legislatures. In its defense, the industry coalition used institutional dimensions prominent in the United States—commercial speech protections rooted in constitutional law and policy preemption based on national supremacy—to reassert policy subsystem dominance. The food industry challenged state laws with a venue shift to courts and then Congress when the courts didn't act swiftly or decisively. The venue shifts from states and courts to a federal legislative solution was led by the food industry, despite past efforts to limit federal label regulations beyond nutritional and ingredient information.

Industry dynamics and public attention to the labeling debate brought increased pressure on lawmakers to find a national solution. Mandatory GMO labeling bills had been introduced in half of the nation's states and reintroduced in subsequent years after close losses. Activists won mandatory labeling laws in Connecticut, Maine, and Vermont, states with strong environmental, small-scale dairy, and organic food producer interests. The first two had trigger mechanisms requiring similar laws in neighboring states to become effective. Under pressure to defend their fishing industry and heritage, Oregon debated and Alaska passed a mandatory labeling law after FDA approved AquAdvantage salmon "as safe to eat as any non-genetically engineered (GE) Atlantic salmon." A narrow labeling requirement for GE-salmon was inserted into a December 2015 spending bill. Consumerist movements had grown in progressive areas and states. Consumerist approaches by anti-GMO groups disrupted markets and created new competitive dynamics among producers and grocers. Several grocery chains, including Kroger, Whole Foods, Safeway, Target, and Trader Joe's, pledged not to sell GE seafood while the FDA considered approval of genetically-engineered salmon. Voluntary labeling and "GMO free" certifications became a competitive opportunity for organic and natural food producers, grocers, and restaurants to differentiate themselves and appeal to consumers, particularly in areas with "foodie" cultures and higher incomes. Food companies including Campbell's, Mars, and Dannon committed to explicitly labeling GMOs on their products. Over the past several years, large food and consumer products companies purchased natural and organic companies, including Unilever's purchase of Ben and Jerry's, General Mills' acquisition of Annie's Organics, Kellogg's purchase of Kashi, and PepsiCo's buy of Naked Juice. Food industry giants now had complicated economic interests in brands and products containing GM ingredients, as well as products that didn't. Consumers' willingness to pay more for organic and non-GMO foods presented a market opportunity that could be exploited with voluntary labeling. Industry labeling positions also shifted under pressure by anti-GM groups to stop funding anti-labeling initiative campaigns or face boycotts.

The legislation also shows industry's effort to co-opt GM labeling by challenging the "Non- GMO Project verified" label widely recognized by consumers. Industry responded to consumerist "right to know" demands by pushing market and technology approaches to convey product information. In December 2015, GMA introduced a "SmartLabel" initiative based on QR codes that consumers scan with their smartphones. Market and technology approaches to providing information keep labeling decisions in private decision venues dominated by producers and grocers with advantages over consumers. Producers and grocers control how much to disclose and its presentation while consumers must seek out information and make assessments across many food choices. The prominent "Non-GMO Project Verified" butterfly-themed seal might be replaced with a new standard digital practice that conveyed little on-package information. Consumer Reports (2014) found the Non-GMO Project certification to be the only "highly meaningful" label for consumers trying to avoid GMOs, out-ranking organic labels.

By early 2016, many companies started to label GM foods nationwide as the easiest way to comply with the impending Vermont law. It was "too complex and expensive to create a separate distribution network" and they wanted to demonstrate responsiveness to increasingly mobilized consumers. ConAgra used social media to communicate its belief that consumers should know what's in their food and said it "supports using a variety of options for disclosure of GMOs." Kellogg also announced its products with GMOs would have labels nationwide to comply with the Vermont law, but only "until a federal solution is reached" (Gasparro, 2016). Brands that embraced digital disclosures, QR codes rather than consumer-facing labels, were and are subjected to food activist pressure. Hershey was a large target of an Organic Consumers Association campaign. The diversity of industry responses and complaints about perceived inconsistency and inequity under the Vermont law sharpened the focus of Congress on finding a "uniform" labeling solution. The GMA argued Vermont's law exempted "60% of food products" so consumers could not be sure that all GM foods were labeled. The only sure option to avoid GM foods was to buy products labeled "USDA certified organic" (Bailey 2015).

Industry was unable to win an injunction to stop Vermont's law in May 2015, although it had previously found success in federal court venues. In a risky but decisive venue, the food industry pushed Congress to act, to initiate several versions of preemptive labeling legislation, and ultimately to reach a compromise. The threat of Vermont's GM labeling law going into effect on July 1, 2016 can be seen as an agenda setting "trigger event" that focused attention on industry concerns and favored action (Cobb and Elder 1972). In mid-April 2016, biotechnology interests, for example, amassed a "fly-in" to lobby Congress. Lobbying reports showed a 31% jump in "GMO lobbying" among 64 companies, trade groups and advocacy organizations (Bloomberg 2016). Senate bill sponsor Pat Roberts (R-KS) worked out a compromise bill with Senator Lisa Murkowski (D-AK) on the Agriculture, Nutrition, and Forestry Committee by summer 2016, but not in time to stop compliance labeling by several companies. Ultimately, food industry allies dominated legislation for the new national disclosure policy innovation, and also won a government-sponsored consumer education program to promote bioengineered-food.

Narrative policy analysis focuses on advocates' framing of policy problems, including how they are understood, defined, categorized, and measured. Deborah Stone's work on political decision-making distinguishes between rational-maximizing models and an empirically-derived "polis model" characterized by "reasoning by metaphor and analogy." Groups use narrative stories about change and power, with symbols, heroes, and villains to define problems and policy solutions. Their narrative framing focuses on winners and losers, who bears costs versus who benefits, and the magnification or diminishment of scientific uncertainty. In the polis model, information that policy depends upon is "ambiguous, interpretive, incomplete, and strategically manipulated." Groups' strategic portrayals intended for persuasion in policy are key forms of power (Stone 2012, 11-12). Pro and anti-labeling coalitions used economic and power narratives in the GM labeling policy debate. Their frames focused on speech rights, consumer rights, threats to producers and consumers, food costs, and food safety, with competing portrayals.

Advocacy coalition narratives in legal venues emerged in milk labeling cases starting in the 1990s, when competing groups tried to require or prohibit labeling milk products from cows treated with genetically-engineered hormones (Keel 2014). The environmental food and agricultural coalition again challenged industry dominance of the federal food policy subsystem in the Obama era with anti-GM narratives that succeeded in mobilizing and securing legislation for mandatory GM food labelling in several states, but not nationally. Activist groups increased the saliency of GM food risk and mobilized public outcry through social media, online and offline organizing, and lobbying, particularly in state legislatures where they could compete with industry. The anti-GM environmental coalition chose state legislatures and ballot initiatives venues based on their democratic-populist ideological preferences and organizational strengths. They advocated popular themes of consumer choice, right to know, and the protection of local producers, including organics. Their campaigns linked rights framing to a narrative of the agriculture industry, particularly Monsanto, as the villain, wielding monopoly power, harming smaller producers, and risking public and environmental health. The food industry, including grocers, was portrayed as complicit in promoting GM foods without consumer knowledge or consent. The biotech–agriculture-food industry coalition met threats to their policy dominance in several venues. They were able to narrowly defeat ballot initiatives in several western states by redefining the debate in negative ads and focusing on economic frames that emphasized short-term costs to consumers.

Narrative analysis theory in political communications distinguishes between generic and issue-specific framings, based on different levels of abstraction. This distinction is useful for political analysis of narratives crafted by advocates, which are then reflected or reframed by policymakers and media. Generic frames provide a context for the policy debate and reflect broadly-held values appealing to policymakers, for example, frames focused on "commerce' or "informing consumers' in the GMO debates. Generic frames may be used by both sides of a debate for different interpretation, which can challenge content analysis methods (Brüggemann and D'Angelo 2018). Generic frames from industry and FDA about the importance of informing consumers meant appropriate communication that didn't imply difference or risk in genetically-engineered foods and food inputs. For the labeling advocacy coalition, informing meant consumers' right to full GMO disclosure, and labeling that did provide a justifiable warning. Issue-specific frames can be powerful "taglines' with embedded values that are used individually or linked together to shape opinion (Nelson and Willey 2001). Advocates draw distinctions in problem definition and promote specific provisions or actions over others in policy debates. In this case, "patchwork of laws' became a tagline founded on economic efficiency values that promoted, even necessitated, the preemptive federal law alternative. Policymakers pick up and repeat issue-specific frames, signaling colleagues and interest groups about their values and priorities. Professional journalists covering biotechnology and food policy debates choose among issue-specific frames to report. Examination of stories in the *New York Times* and *Wall Street Journal* during the 2014-2016 congressional debates show coverage of a generic "consumer interest' frame with industry's commerce and science narratives highlighted. Labeling advocates' rights and risks narratives were not prominent among elite news outlets. Content analysis of online sources that shape and reflect public opinion would likely show more of the rights and risks frames; these concerns were prominent in the lay public comments during USDA rulemaking after the law passed.

Narrative policy analysis of groups' competitive framing of the GM labeling problem and preferred solutions across and within venues illuminates the policy development that extended national labeling authority and undid nascent state GM labeling laws. By analyzing the range of generic and issue-specific frames used in their narratives, we can see the rationales for policy change embraced by policymakers and woven into the legislation and its implementation.

REGULATORY FEDERALISM

Agriculture and related biotech and food industries have secured promotional policies in production, distribution, and marketing within established but contested regulatory regimes. In regulatory conflict, the goals of each advocacy coalition have been clear. Environmental groups historically sought to restrict the spread of genetically engineered seeds, foods, and ingredients in the fields and markets. GMO protestors and labeling advocates, in turn, launched a movement and raised funds and issue awareness nationally to challenge the agricultural and food industries' advantage in national policymaking. GM food labeling as a policy alternative was pursued after opponents failed in the existing USDA and FDA regulatory regimes to limit broad application of genetic engineering in agriculture and food production, including insect-resistant corn and soybeans, herbicide-tolerant sugar beets, and, most recently, GE-salmon. Environmental groups didn't get far advocating for mandatory GM labels in federal agencies. The introduction and marketing of genetically-modified plants and seeds has faced few restrictions from the USDA. Corporate agricultural-biotechnology and food industries have long promoted market freedom within an established regulatory regime that identifies GMOs as "Generally Recognized as Safe" (GRAS) and establishes labeling guidelines that prohibit misleading consumers. These industries have leveraged market-liberal institutional power to protect and expand their production and sale of GM foods, notably since approval of the FLAVR SAVR tomato in 1994. Their institutional power is founded on legal constraints on regulators, and commercial and scientific dominance in policymaking that encourages agency cooperation with industry interests.

The Federal Food, Drug, and Cosmetic Act (1938) and Nutrition Labeling and Education Act (1990) authorizes the FDA to regulate nutrition and health labeling on prepared and packaged foods and beverages, with goals to inform consumers and prevent them from being misled. Raw foods, fruits, vegetables and fish can be voluntarily labeled with nutrition information. Food "structure and function' claims on conventional food labels must be "truthful and not misleading" under the law, but the ability to isolate, add, and modify foods and food components through biotechnology complicates application of that standard. Within USDA, the Food

Safety and Inspection Service (FSIS) is responsible for safety of meat, poultry, and egg products and has authority in labeling and packaging. The National Organic Program regulates the standards for agricultural products marketed as organically produced, a program many small producers see as too onerous for their participation and favoring large corporate agribusinesses and food companies. Each of these agencies must work with food growers, manufacturers, and sellers, prompting environmental group concerns that commercial interests dominate the relationship.

Dominant agriculture science has demonstrated the "substantial equivalence' of bioengineered foods. The Food and Drug Administration positions on food product safety and labeling rules are based on substantial equivalence, which has created a regulatory environment favorable to GM producers and the food industry. FDA approvals and agency rulemaking regularly conflicted with activist demands for more process and product information on labels to address environmental, health, and welfare concerns. They denied a 2011 Center for Food Safety "Citizen Petition" calling for change in FDA policy to require GMO labeling on behalf of organic producers and food companies. FDA has repeatedly denied authority to require the mandatory GM food labels, stating science finds "no material difference' between non-GM and GM food products. The FDA approved GE farm-raised salmon without a labeling requirement in November 2015 and they argued, "FDA can only require additional labeling of foods derived from GE sources if there is a material difference—such as a different nutritional profile" (FDA 2015). In November 2015, they promulgated *guidances* for voluntary labeling of food derived from GE plants and GE salmon, following-up on a 2001 guidance for voluntary labeling bioengineered foods. The agency consistently resisted expanded responsibilities for mandatory national labeling, from their 1992 *Statement of Policy: Foods Derived from New Plant Varieties* up to the 2016 disclosure debates in Congress (FDA 1992).

In 1993, the Food & Drug Administration approved genetically-engineered bovine growth hormone, known as recombinant Bovine Somatotropin (rbST), for treating dairy cows to increase milk volume. FDA found dairy products from treated cows "indistinguishable' from untreated cows. Subsequent protective labeling "guidances' constrained disclosure and "production claims' on food labels to industry's benefit (Kysar 2004). FDA's 2001 *Guidance for Industry: Voluntary Labeling Indicating Whether Foods Have or have Not Been Developed Using Bioengineering* cautioned against mandatory GM labels and promoted appropriate voluntary labels. For example, milk from cows treated with Monsanto's recombinant Bovine Somatotropin (rBST), also known as recombinant Bovine Growth Hormone (rGBH), did not require disclosure. Further, FDA advised that milk producers should not make label claims of "rBST-free", a compositional claim that could mislead consumers, but should instead use "from cows not treated with rbST" and include the disclaimer "No significant difference has been shown between milk derived from rbST-treated and non-rbST-treated cows." The guidance was updated in 2015 and 2019 to discourage "GMO free," "GE free," "does not contain GMOs," and "non- GMO" label statements, and to promote language "not genetically modified through the use of modern biotechnology" or a similar process statement (FDA 2019). Industry pointed to agency guidances to support their narratives decrying "compelled speech' as misleading to consumers in federal courts. Agency support for the food industry's commercial and consumer information narrative frames is also reflected in House and Senate hearings and letters they submitted to the Senate Agriculture Committee.

The U.S. Department of Agriculture's promotional relationships with the farmers, agri-biotech, and food industries is well established through its Agricultural Marketing Service, and its mission to "support the country's diverse agricultural operations" and "create domestic and international marketing opportunities" (USDA 2019). In 2015, responding to producer interests, AMS announced a voluntary certification program for food companies to pay to have their products labeled "G.M.O.-free" despite FDA's long opposition to such label language. When industry chose to pursue preemptive federal legislation, the USDA supported their expanded regulatory roles, including labeling options to serve producer and consumer needs, and marketing to educate consumers about the benefits of biotechnology.

FEDERAL COURTS AS A POLICY VENUE

The First Amendment of the U.S. Constitution, limits legislative power regarding speech, including commercial speech. Commercial speech is protected unless it is judged false or misleading, so government must demonstrate a significant state interest to restrict it. Federal courts have linked commercial speech freedom to listeners' rights and consumers' interests, principles explored in milk labeling cases and reflected in the litigants' narratives. In *Bigelow* (1975), the U.S. Supreme Court rejected advertising restrictions and articulated a consumer's right to receive information, and in *Virginia Pharmacy* (1976) it endorsed a "consumer's interest in the free flow of information."[1] The Constitution also protects the right not to speak, which increases court scrutiny of product labeling mandates. The federal courts have employed varying levels of scrutiny to laws and regulations limiting commercial speech, and evolving case law has created uncertainty regarding the government's burden. In two cases of labeling milk derived from cows treated with rbST, federal courts applied stricter scrutiny and state labeling regulations were struck down as violating commercial free speech.

Federal Circuit Court rulings in the *International Dairy Foods v. Amestoy* (1996) and *IDFA v. Boggs* (2010)[2] created legal barriers to labeling genetically-altered agricultural products while reinforcing corporate free speech rights. IDFA, a "big-dairy" interest group, successfully persuaded the courts to strike down a Vermont law and an Ohio regulation. The rigorous test of power to restrict commercial speech is articulated in the Supreme Court case *Central Hudson Gas and Electric v. Public Service Commission* (1980)[3], and the case was invoked in circuit courts' decisions on milk labeling. The *Central Hudson* test includes four

[1] Bigelow v. Commonwealth of Virginia, 421 U.S. 809 (1975); Virginia State Board of Pharmacy v. Citizen's Consumer Council, Inc. 425 US 748 (1976).
[2] *International Dairy Foods v. Amestoy*, 92 F. 3d 67 (2nd Circuit, 1996); *IDFA v. Boggs*, 622 F. 3d 628 (6th Circuit, 2010).
[3] *Central Hudson Gas and Electric v. Public Service Commission.* 447 U.S. 557 (1980).

prongs: (1) the commercial speech must concern lawful activity and not be misleading to be protected; (2) the government must demonstrate a "substantial interest' in regulating the speech; (3) the government must show that the regulation "directly serves the interest;' finally, (4) the regulation must be "no more extensive than necessary' to advance the state interest. The circuit courts' application of the *Central Hudson* test had great policy implications by requiring regulators to produce evidence that their rules would achieve policy goals with the least burden on commercial speech rights.

The *Central Hudson* test was applied in the *Amestoy* case, where the 2nd Circuit Court found Vermont had failed to establish a "substantial state interest" in labeling rbST-produced milk. Vermont regulators argued that the state labeling mandate was intended to provide information that consumers wanted and had a "right to know.' The circuit court recognized the trial record evidence of consumer interest in milk production process and public concerns about FDA's rbST safety determination, as well as concerns about effects on bovine health and the economic well-being of the state's dairy farms. But the State's justification of promoting consumer information was deemed insufficient. In controversial language, the majority opinion stated that "consumer curiosity" about the milk production process was inadequate to justify state interest and compel "even an accurate, factual statement" (*Amestoy*, 55). The court relied on the FDA's 2001 *Voluntary Labeling Interim Guidance* to diminish public health concerns asserted by Vermont. The state had not established that the labeling regulation addressed a real harm because the record contained "no scientific evidence from which an objective observer could conclude that rbST has any impact at all on dairy products" (*Amestoy*, 33-34). The mandatory labeling rule failed the second prong of the *Central Hudson* test.

Circuit Judge Leval wrote in a strong dissent that Vermont's regulation was based on substantial state interests of human and cow health, survival of small farms, and concerns about manipulating nature. He also argued that the First Amendment favors the flow of "accurate, relevant information" in commercial speech and milk producers fighting the labeling requirement were seeking "concealment" despite their "self-righteous references to free expression" (*Amestoy*, 77). Judge Leval criticized the majority for omitting important facts in the record and distorting the policy purpose. In his view, the Vermont Agriculture Department's Economic Impact Statement had established health and safety concerns of consumers and threats to the economic well-being of dairy farms facing milk surplus. The dissent reflected a precautionary philosophy allowing states to adopt regulations more cautious than the FDA's under conditions of scientific uncertainty. But Vermont failed to argue a position on whether rbST was beneficial or detrimental; they based state interest arguments on the consumer's right to know, rather than health harms (Kysar 2004).

Over the next several years, dairy processors began to expand sourcing and labeling milk from cows not treated with rbST in response to consumer demand. In 2008, Ohio Governor Strickland used an executive order to compel label regulation in conformity with FDA guidances. The Ohio Department of Agriculture created an administrative rule that prohibited labeling milk with compositional claims including "No Hormones," "Hormone Free," "rbST free," "rbGH free," "No Artificial Hormones" and "bst-free," because these claims were "false and misleading." ODA also prohibited using the phrase "this milk is from cows not supplemented with rbST" unless it was accompanied by a disclosure on the same label panel stating, "FDA has determined no significant difference has been shown between milk derived from rbST-supplemented and non-supplemented cows" (Ohio 2008). The state intended to put production claims "into context' as recommended by FDA. The rules were challenged in federal district court in two lawsuits brought by the International Dairy Foods Association and by the Organic Trade Association, representing specialty and smaller dairy interests. The district court combined the cases and ruled in favor of the state. In *IDFA v. Boggs*, the 6th Circuit Court reviewed the First Amendment challenges to the state's ban on milk composition claims and the state's disclosure requirement for production claims. The court struck down the labeling prohibition as an unconstitutional ban on commercial speech: "the Rule does not directly advance the State's interest and is more extensive than necessary to serve that interest" (*Boggs*, 639). The dairy industry won recognition of freedom to voluntarily label, but the decision also recognized scientific evidence challenging the FDA's "no material difference' finding in milk from treated and untreated cows. The two cases left unsettled whether states might yet construct a GMO labeling law that could survive judicial review (Keel 2014).

The constitutionality of Vermont's 2014 law was challenged in *Grocery Manufacturers Association v. Sorrell* in the U.S. Court of Appeals for the Second Circuit.[4] Interested parties and legal scholars debated the level of scrutiny under which the compulsory labeling law would be evaluated (Sundar 2015). A rational basis burden, found in the Supreme Court's *Zauderer* decision, establishes a test of "purely factual and uncontroversial information" for mandating disclosure.[5] Industry has argued for tougher intermediate scrutiny based on the *Central Hudson* case, requiring "service of a substantial governmental interest, and only through means that directly advance that interest" to regulate commercial speech, which the court applied in the *Amestoy* case. Vermont and its allies argued that the GM labeling law would withstand scrutiny even if *Amestoy* was invoked because the state had established a substantial health and welfare interest. In November 2015, the 2nd Circuit refused to grant industry's request for an injunction to stop the law from going into effect July 1, 2016 while the court reviewed the case. The legal arguments presented by GMA and conservative legal allies reflected many of the commercial "free speech' narratives of prior cases and new narratives promoting preemption under existing federal labeling law and regulation. Legal questions about the appropriate level of scrutiny and policy means were not resolved; the new BE disclosure law made the case moot.

LEGISLATIVE DEBATES AND GM POLICY NARRATIVES

Policy streams depend on attention, problem framing, policy alternatives, and incentives for policymakers, which the food industry provided in this case. They

---

[4] Grocery Manufacturers Association et al v. Sorrell et al, Docket Number: 15-1504 (2nd Circuit, 2015).
[5] Zauderer v. Office of Disciplinary Counsel, 471 U.S. 626 (1985).

came to Congress with a clear and immediate problem framed in ways relevant to favored constituencies, and industry worked to shape the policy alternatives in the legislation and administrative rulemaking. Congress took up national labeling policy reform only after state initiatives threatened the status quo policy subsystem. The 2014-2016 legislative debate about voluntary or mandatory labeling of genetically modified or bioengineered foods, and why or whether to preempt state laws demonstrates the dominance of the food industry's narrative story. Industry chose the national legislative venue to preempt Vermont's law and pushed Republican leadership to protect its status quo labeling control from imminent threat of explicit GM labeling enforcement in the summer of 2016. They had successfully defeated threats from GM labeling ballot initiatives and would enlist many of the same frames of urgency and economic dangers to incite congressional leaders to act. Deborah Stone (2012) likens words to weapons in the problem definition arsenal. Problem definition matters because views are extremely sensitive to language (Tversky and Kahneman 1981). Industry's commercial frames provided more compelling narratives about threats, villains, and appropriate national policy solutions, even as the preemptive legislation evolved from a voluntary GM labeling law to a mandatory bioengineering disclosure with options.

The food industry's narrative story for "defining and contesting policy" (Stone, 158) took aim at the opposition's powerful "right to know' consumer-oriented generic framing with specific issues frames highlighting dangers of misleading labels on safe, bioengineered foods. Opponents of preemption, those that sought mandatory, front-facing GMO labeling, saw their "right to know' narrative minimized and reframed to a concern for "appropriate' consumer information. Vermont was cast as villain for its "unilateral' actions and the mandatory GM label law was characterized as dangerous and inequitable. If allowed to take effect, labels would "mislead consumers' about genetic engineering, implying difference and risk, and wrongly dissuade them from safe food products. In a *Wall Street Journal* opinion piece in May 2015, Grocery Manufacturers Association President argued Vermont should not be allowed "to ignore scientific consensus on GMOs" and producers and consumers should be protected as "labels will be misconstrued as warnings" (Bailey 2015).

Industry dominated problem definition in language tailored to congressional authority and interests, highlighting fears for interstate commerce and price hikes for food producers and consumers. They and refocused the debate onto generic economic frames, emphasizing problems for "producers and consumers' and issue-specific frames focusing on claims that Vermont's mandatory labeling would harm interstate commerce, create compliance burdens and "legal risk' for food companies and grocers, and drive up "food costs' for the country. The GMA president also warned food distribution "complexities will explode" if producers and grocers had to "separate GMO products from non-GMO products." GMA again emphasized claims made in negative ads to defeat labeling initiatives in several states, namely that the law would "increase grocery costs for families by $500 a year" (Bailey 2015).

Industry's success in dominating the debate is demonstrated by lawmakers' adoption of industry's talking points in bill language and public communications, as detailed below. Opponents of preemption, those that sought mandatory, front-facing

GMO labeling, saw their narrative of "right to know' minimized and reframed to a concern for appropriate consumer information. The food industry and Republican lawmakers in the House and Senate defined problems using generic frames as "symbolic devices" (Stone, 159). They promoted and reinforced beliefs in American agricultural superiority, innovation, and global dependence upon it to address human and environmental problems. Industry and its allies linked these generic frames to issue-specific battle metaphors defending of "sound science' and food production systems. Vermont's label law threatened disaster for producers forced to mislead consumers into thinking bad thoughts about GE foods. Vermont's label requirements would stymie "progress' of genetic food technology that farmers needed to face resource challenges and feed the burgeoning world. Symbolic threat framing allowed elected representatives to claim credit for a law to protect consumer interests, provide appropriate knowledge about product ingredients to enhance consumer choice, and keep food prices low. Influential American Farm Bureau Federation President agreed with congressional narratives he helped inspire, "This bill is not perfect, but it would avoid the chaos of 50 different state laws and a confusing array of labels for ingredients scientifically proven safe" (Haddon 2016).

HOUSE ANALYSIS

Industry created the "Coalition for Safe Affordable Food," with members from Grocery Manufacturers Association, Biotechnology Industry Association, and corn, soybean, and beet sugar associations. They fiercely lobbied for the bill and saw its passage through the House. Representative Pompeo of Kansas, member of the House Committee on Energy and Commerce, sponsored the "Safe and Accurate Food Labeling Act" to establish a national *voluntary* GMO label standard in 2014. The bill title defines the policy problem with industry frames about the safety of GMOs, and the use of "accurate" labeling reasserts industry and FDA positions that "GMO-free" label statements alone can be misleading without more contextual information. The bill also included a process for securing a government "USDA verified" GMO-free label statement which some meat and egg producers wanted for competitive opportunities. Pompeo argued from the beginning that genetic engineering is "a perfectly safe technology" that didn't need labeling, but national voluntary labeling was necessitated by "loud opposition" and "commercial interest" (Frank 2015). He repeatedly vowed to protect Kansas farmers and serve industry goals to stop state mandatory labeling laws, avoid expensive campaigns to defeat state initiatives, and reduce "fear-mongering' about GM foods. Table 1 illustrates the most frequently used phrases and framings in the House Agriculture Committee's report on the bill.

Labeling advocates who defended Vermont's approach referred to the House bill as the "DARK" Act, denying Americans' right to know. Labeling advocates' popular right to know narrative was embraced at the state level in Vermont, bolstered by ideas of local food sovereignty and heritage food production. Media coverage and social media activity reflected a broader debate about consumer rights, safety, and disputes over science than the legislative discourses. The most common frame in New York Times and Wall Street Journal articles and opinion pieces

(40%) focused on informing consumers. The second and third most common frames concerned science (32%) and commerce (25%). These generic frames often included issue-specific concern for consumer understanding of genetic engineering; "poor public understanding of the science" was a frame picked up and repeated by the *New York Times*, for example (Brody 2015). In the congressional debates, consumerist narratives of right to know were redirected along with their favored strict policy of full GM disclosure on the food or package. Vermont labeling advocates framed the issue as a rights problem, but it became reframed as an information problem. "Transparency,' idealized by labeling advocates, became part of the problem in congressional debates. Legislative leaders sided with industry and agency narratives that consumers might be misled about the safety and benefits of GM foods. The debate began to center around congressional and industry efforts to promote safe, "bioengineered" foods and appropriately informing rather than denying consumers food information. State interests and traditions in regulating health and welfare under federalism were largely absent in the debate. While proponents of Vermont's law asserted that democratically elected representatives at the state level passed legislation important to residents, such actions were portrayed as unilateral and harmful to national commerce, even harmful to global human development and environmental interests.

Table 1: Most Frequent Phrases, Concepts, and Frames in House Agriculture Committee Report (HR 1599)

Phrases and Concepts by Frequency	Narrative Frames

• Agri- biotechnology
   o Agricultural production
   o Genetically engineered inputs
   o Scientific consensus (safety, wise use)
	• Production Benefit
	• Scientific Progress

• Misinformation on safety o Confusing to consumers	• Communication

• Food supply
   o Disruption
   o Food costs
	• Interstate Commerce
	• Distribution Harm
	• Consumer Harm

• State by state patchwork of laws
   o Unilateral labeling law
   o Vermont specific labels
	• Interstate Commerce
	• Equity

• Ever growing population • Grow more food with less (water, land, energy)	• Global Challenges • Environment • Scientific Progress

• Food supply chain
   o Segregate, separate
   o Higher costs for farmers, manufacturers, consumers
	• Distribution Harm
	• Producers and Consumers

Defending genetically engineered foods as safe was a clear priority in the House legislation. The narratives of GM food critics had mobilized activists but not most policymakers. Opponents of GMOs in food and food production have long questioned the scientific consensus on GMO safety. They originally focused on health risks from consuming GM foods, which cultivated public concern, unfounded concern from the perspectives of the dominant policy subsystem leaders. "Scientific consensus' was repeatedly invoked by lawmakers who referred to FDA findings and a timely May 2016 National Academies of Science report on GE crops and food safety. Critics shifted to narratives emphasizing environmental risks from increased glyphosate pesticide exposure in consumers and agricultural communities and purity threats to organic food production. More radical criticisms of biotechnology continue to include genetic pollution and unnatural, un-Godly manipulation of life, but they did not penetrate the congressional discourses. Environmental concerns most often invoked by lawmakers mapped to those long asserted by industry. Genetically engineered crops and foods would reduce environmental degradation by reducing pesticide use, increasing yields, and using less water, land, and energy. The language used in the House report reflects the pro-environmental and scientific progress framing that the agri-biotechnology industry has long promoted. By late 2015, the pro-biotech Genetic Literacy Project proclaimed that fear-mongering was waning in a *Wall Street Journal* op-ed entitled "March of Genetic Food Progress" (Kelly 2015).

Consumer information was clearly a secondary goal to protecting biotechnology in the House debate. The definition of GM food was narrowed under the law to recombinant DNA (r-DNA) technology to reduce the scope of regulation and shield industry "innovations" such as increasingly successful gene-editing techniques. The legislation expanded federal agency authority for safety reviews of products engineered with "new traits" and only mandated labels if unsafe. These provisions appeared largely symbolic, not a rational effort to increase regulatory risk assessment and address food safety fears. An appropriate regulatory response to unsafe food would not be labeling but rejecting products. Labeling advocates warned that narrow applicability would reduce accuracy and safety, not advance it.

The dominant narratives in Congress relied on a machine metaphor, the food production system, that could be harmed or broken by bad state GM label laws. This metaphor was promoted first by the food industry in their commerce narratives. The Grocery Manufacturers Association called attention to the growing threat of labeling laws introduced in 20 states: "The system could become a patchwork mess with each state developing unique definitions, loopholes, and enforcement mechanisms." GMA endorsed the House bill's delegation of authority to agency control where "FDA retains authority over the establishment of uniform, science-based labeling" (Bailey 2015). In July 2015, the House passed the bill with bi-partisan support, 275-150 votes. Agriculture Committee Chairman Conaway declared in a July 23rd press release, "H.R. 1599 establishes a voluntary nation-wide marketing program that gives consumers access to consistent, reliable information while protecting advancements in food production technology and innovation."

Production system harm was sometimes characterized by lawmakers as inadvertent or "misguided" and other times as intentional—the most powerful narrative offense strategy according to Stone (209). Bill sponsor Pompeo demonstrated intentional harm language in press release after the law was passed: "Radical, anti-science advocates...will no longer have the ability to disrupt the market and raise food prices" (Pompeo 2016). He claimed credit for preventing "misguided state and local food labeling laws...devastating for Kansas farmers, rural communities, and families." Framing the problem as systemic with easily identifiable causes and bad actors made congressional action seem imperative and their favored course of action necessary.

SENATE ANALYSIS

The Senate wrote their bill to amend the Agricultural Marketing Act of 1946 and ultimately required the USDA to develop a new "national bioengineered food disclosure standard." Senate Agriculture Committee Chair Pat Roberts (R-KS) and Ranking Member Debbie Stabenow (D-MI) repeatedly described the main problem in similar terms, as a "state by state patchwork" and "50-state patchwork of regulations" while differing in narrative tone. Table 2, listing the most frequently used phrases and frames from the committee's hearings report, displays a broader range of narratives than the committee's final bill report displayed in Table 3.

The Senate debate reflected similar narratives to those in the House, using market, producer, and consumer frames, but the language from Senators was more moderated. Notably, within their scientific progress framing, Republican language shifted away from the politicized term "genetic engineering" to the more benign term biotechnology. There was less focus on safety as the debate had narrowed to a market problem and communication solution focus. They did not demonize labeling advocates as some industry and House Representatives had, but they divided label advocates with a weak mandatory disclosure bill. Certified organics producers benefitted, for example, and were authorized to use "not bioengineered" claims on their labels.

In October 2015 "stakeholder hearings," the chairman articulated a dire narrative to *protect* the "value chain of agriculture and food production" and *protect* farmers who must "produce more safe and affordable food" in the face of production challenges. Senator Roberts warned of "global security threats" tied to food shortages and price increases. He focused on land and water resource limits, uncertain weather, and pests and diseases that challenged farmers and he characterized agriculture biotechnology as a "valuable tool" that must be defended. Senator Stabenow also wanted to address concerns from "our farmers, our food companies, [and] our consumers" but called for maintaining the "nation's agricultural leadership" in more positive language. She repeatedly referred to "innovation" and the desire to promote "safe, beneficial" biotechnology to "help solve dual global challenges of climate change and global food security" (Senate 2016a).

Senator Stabenow set forth a test for any bi-partisan labeling solution in the October 2015 hearings, reiterating that the bill had to address the "patchwork of laws' problem and create "a national system of disclosure and transparency for consumers" but one that "does not stigmatize biotechnology." She was responsive to consumer and environmental pressures for GM disclosure, but she strongly defended American farmers and ranchers as the best in the world producing the most abundant and safest food supply. Stabenow supported industry and agriculture science efforts to promote biotechnology, "to build better confidence in these technologies so that all consumers better understand their benefits" (Senate 2016a).

In his opening remarks to the committee in March 2016, Roberts asserted that a patchwork of laws was "disrupting the interstate flow of agriculture and food products in our nation's marketplace" even though Vermont was the only state with an impending law. He sidelined anti-GM food narrative frames when declaring the problem was "not a safety or health issue. It is a market issue" (Senate 2016b). Chairman Roberts warned "threat to the technology hurts the entire value chain—from farmer to consumer" in the committee's mark-up report. While summarizing provisions, the report reiterated threats to commerce framing and the need for a national disclosure standard "designed to solely address marketing matters, not based on any concerns with respect to safety of bioengineered foods or ingredients" (Senate 2016c). He also implicated Vermont's law when saying to the *New York Times,* "We can't demonize food with unnecessary labels" (Steinhauer 2016). But Democratic Senators were divided over whether disclosure would really be mandatory. Senator Jon Tester (D-MT), an organic farmer, argued against the bill because, "Voluntary standards are no standards at all."

Table 2: Most Frequent Phrases, Concepts, and Frames in Senate Agriculture, Nutrition, and Forestry Hearings Report (S. Hrg. 114-261)

Phrases and Concepts by Frequency	Narrative Frames
• Genetically engineered, bioengineered	• Production Benefit • Scientific Progress
• Preempt state and Local o Mandate labeling	• Intergovernmental

• National disclosure
   o Standard, requirement
   o Uniform
	• Intergovernmental
	• Communication

• Human Food o Agriculture and food products	• Agricultural Production • Consumer Benefit
• Marketplace, market issue	• Interstate Commerce

• State by state patchwork of laws
   o Unilateral labeling law of VT
   o Vt specific labels
	• Interstate Commerce
	• Equity

• Ever growing population • Grow more food with less (water, land, energy)	• Global Challenges • Environment • Scientific Progress

• Food supply chain
   o Segregate, separate
   o Higher costs for farmers, manufacturers, consumers
	• Distribution Harm
	
	• Producer and Consumer Harm

Table 3: Most Frequent Phrases, Related Concepts, and Frames in Senate Agriculture, Nutrition, and Forestry Committee Report (S. 114-403)

Phrases and Concepts by Frequency	Narrative Frames
• Bioengineered, genetic	• Production Benefit

o Science, scientific		•	Scientific Progress
• Product, produce		•	Production
• Disclosure, labeling		•	Communication
• Market, marketing o Costs, distribution		•	Interstate Commerce
• Safe, safety		•	Risk
• Consistent, consistency		•	Interstate Commerce

FRAMING LEGISLATIVE OUTCOMES

The Senate bill initially failed to pass due to division among Democrats, and labeling advocates claimed victory prematurely. Industry pressure won the day. The compromise bill with mandatory if flexible disclosure passed in time to preempt implementation of Vermont's law.

After the June compromise bill was passed, Republican and Democratic Senators claimed credit for saving constituent groups. Chairman Roberts announced, "We saved agricultural biotechnology." Ranking Member Stabenow (D-MI) characterized the "national mandatory label for food products that contain genetically modified ingredients" as "a win for consumers and families" (Brasher 2016). Democrats succeeded in amending the original bill from a voluntary to a mandatory disclosure standard with their intensive mobilization around the "right to know' narrative. Even though the final legislation was altered, Representative Pompeo reasoned that regulation of interstate commerce would be light and "permit the government to stay out of the way of these consumer choices," thus reducing government interference while increasing national authority (House 2016). Chairman Roberts lauded Section 294 of the bill that "directs the USDA to provide science-based education, outreach, and promotion" (Senate 2016c). Environmental groups viewed this provision as an industry propaganda effort to be paid for by the public.

The bioengineering disclosure law is perhaps purposely ambiguous to serve multiple interests and not be offensive to any group. It is telling that both the GMA and Organic Trade Association praised the compromise bill. The standard was left to be specified through USDA rulemaking. The new law required those rules to "prohibit claims regarding the safety or quality of food based on whether or not the food is bioengineered," which protects the food industry and limits the commercial speech of Anti-GM competitors. The labeling mandate was also narrowed to Recombinant DNA techniques of genetic engineering, not controversial gene editing or mutagenesis techniques, which raises new risk assessment concerns among the environmental coalition. Congressional intent to promote marketing of bioengineered foods is a clear policy outcome. USDA must "provide science-based information through education, outreach, and promotion to address consumer acceptance of biotechnology" (Senate 2016d).

The compromise bill excluded restaurants and very small producers from disclosure requirements, allowed various labeling options, including QR codes and phone numbers, which help producers and grocers to retain labeling discretion. The law required USDA to produce a study of electronic and digital disclosure examining consumers' information access problems, as well as a cost-benefit analysis of retail-based scanners to aid consumers. This study provision shows legislators' responsiveness to information access concerns and criticisms of QR codes as inadequate. The law promoted neutral labeling language and prohibited companies from collecting consumer data when they scan or call for food information. These provisions favored consumers, but specific rules would be determined by USDA's Agricultural Marketing Service, such as thresholds of substances requiring disclosure and "other factors and conditions under which food may be labeled as bioengineered." Agency discretion could allow it to favor agri-biotechnology and food industry positions and timetable, an influence that the environmental coalition would counter in the regulatory and judicial venues.

USDA issued a favorable statement touting consumer benefits, arguing the national standard is better than Vermont's law by covering "over 24,000 more products." The agency reflected industry and lawmaker narratives about appropriate communication under BE disclosure that would be "transparent without sending the wrong message about the safety of their food options" (Brasher 2016). The White House supported the bill with language emphasizing science, safety, and consumer information, citing a "broad consensus that foods from genetically engineered crops are safe." President Obama had expressed a pro-labeling position in his campaign and approving the legislation gave him opportunity to follow through and praise "the bipartisan effort to address consumers' interest in knowing more about their food...including genetically engineered crops" (Bloomberg 2016).

NARRATIVE FRAMES IN BE FOOD DISCLOSURE RULEMAKING

In the rulemaking process for BE food disclosure, USDA posed several questions and label image prototypes for public comment. The online database at *Regulations.gov* contains over 14,000 comments submitted to the Agricultural Marketing Service. Final rules would determine whether to require disclosure by processed foods containing refined genetically-engineered oils and corn syrup and what threshold percentage of total product (.9-5%) would trigger disclosure. Rules on the nature and means of disclosure, whether via front of package label with words and symbols, QR code, text message, or web site, also had to be determined. All issues were highly contested by diverse and specialized organizations, trade associations, food companies, and individuals. An initial content analysis of BE frames from advocacy coalitions, trade associations, and corporations is reflected below.

The coalitions were more fractured than during legislative battles. Producer groups reiterated scientific progress frames touting "productivity and efficiency" of American agriculture. Anti-GMO groups continued to advocate consumer "right to know" and full "transparency" to prevent the agri-biotech and foods industries from dominating labeling. As would be expected, more issue-specific narratives emerged about foods or ingredients that would be excluded, disclosure methods, and certification images. As the National Corn Growers Association wrote to AMS, "members of the Coalition have diverging views on mandatory disclosure of refined ingredients, the BE food list, voluntary disclosure, and thresholds" (USDA 2018). Industry groups continued to advocate for a "marketing standard,' not a health standard, thereby preferencing alternatives that were promotional and met their commercial needs.

National agriculture, foods, and trade associations submitted detailed comments including, Grocery Manufacturers Association, International Dairy Foods, American Soybean Association, U.S. Beet Sugar Industry, North American Meat Institute, National Fisheries Institute, American Frozen Foods Institute, Shelf Stable Food Processors Association, and American Bakers Association, as well as companies including Walmart, Coca-Cola, Schwan's, and Sargento. Common industry *progress* narratives emphasized food innovations and environmental benefits, accompanied by *commerce* frames seeking "accurate" labeling and reducing "burden and complexity in the marketplace," as the National Association of Manufacturers put it. The Food Marketing Institute submitted a regulatory impact analysis estimating initial implementation costs at $2.7B-$4B. The high costs were based on oft-articulated concerns for "segregating and separating" BE foods in the "food supply chain." The Chamber of Commerce comments were typical in focusing on BE foods "definition," "appropriate threshold," "refined ingredients," and flexible disclosure "options" with "technology." Many groups seeking exclusions utilized narratives of *production harm,* as did organic groups arguing for higher thresholds. Conventional and organic producers sought to protect their market competitiveness. The New York Farm Bureau promoted member interests in fruit, vegetable, grain, meat, and dairy, some using GM seeds and feed. Their first concerns were for "international competitiveness" and that the standard "not treat bioengineered foods differently" from non-BE foods, a "market discrimination" commerce frame that was repeated by others. They framed the *communication problem* as requiring "completeness" and "accuracy" that could only be achieved with electronic labels.

The National Sustainable Agricultural Coalition and other organic interests advocated for "supply chain independence" and "transparency" of food processes, not just product, because of economic, environmental, and "agronomic impacts" of GE crops. The Center for Food Safety, a large coalition of labeling advocate groups, reasserted polling data showing public support for mandatory labeling and called on the agency to "meet public expectations" and include all food products from genetically-engineered sources and using all genetic engineering techniques. The only alternative acceptable was "clear," "on package" labels "readily accessible to all." They estimated electronic label options would "discriminate against 100 million Americans," primarily rural, low-income, minority, and elderly people who lacked access. Arguing against "bioengineering' as a little-known term, they referred to the "FFDCA standard" of providing label information that would not mislead or confuse consumers. The new law did not require USDA use bioengineered terminology, but industry successfully pushed the term with their *progress* frame.

Just Label It and the Sierra Club launched online petition campaigns to mobilize opposition to industry-friendly rules. Just Label It continued the "denying consumers right to know' theme by casting "Big Ag" as the villain seeking "loopholes" for foods with GMO sugars and oils. They also framed electronic means of disclosure as impractical and inequitable, an effort "targeting the elderly and poor." USDA was portrayed as conspiring with industry by pushing "warm and fuzzy" label images including smiling suns with sunglasses and limited "BE" text. These consumer groups mobilized thousands of people to write for "clear' and "meaningful' labels; many expressed concerns about GMO foods safety and asserted their "right to know' and avoid such foods (USDA 2018).

Deloitte Corporation completed the mandated study on consumer access to disclosure information through electronic and digital methods for AMS. Their findings affirmed concerns about the novel use of digital links for food information, equipment, scanning application, and broadband connection challenges that affected groups disproportionately (Deloitte 2017). This provided evidence to support many of the consumer concerns about "access' and "equity' that were expressed during the comment process, but AMS approved electronic options nonetheless. The report also concluded that, "Language used in current voluntary bioengineering disclosures is not clear or consistent across products, resulting in misunderstanding among interested consumers," which strengthened the dominant "appropriate communication' narrative frames of industry.

AMS finalized the National Bioengineered Food Disclosure Standard in December 2018, followed by an industry fact sheet, webinar, and outreach services (USDA 2019). The webinar asserts that the standard was designed to provide "transparency" for consumers but also to "limit costs" and burdens on industry. Food manufacturers, importers, and retailers who package food or sell it in bulk must disclose bioengineered foods. Meat, poultry and eggs are generally not required to disclose because they are regulated under other statutes, and foods like milk from animals fed BE feed are not considered BE foods. Certified organic foods are excluded. Restaurants and very small food manufacturers are excluded. AMS defined bioengineered foods to those containing genetic material modified by *in vitro* rDNA techniques not obtainable through conventional breeding or "found in nature." If genetic material is "not detectable" it is not bioengineered, and foods with "incidental additives" are not bioengineered (USDA 2019). This means refined foods such as corn syrup from BE corn would not require disclosure, nor would yeasts and enzymes used in baking and brewing. The threshold for inadvertent BE substances is up to 5%, accounting for comingling of BE and non-BE crops. The agency also developed the List of Bioengineered Foods to identify crops and foods available in a bioengineered form, which require disclosure unless they can be demonstrated not to be bioengineered through organic certification or supply chain records. AMS will review the BE foods list annually for updates.

The agency was responsive to industry with four disclosure options and side, top, and front panel placement options. Disclosure by on-package text "Bioengineered Food" or "Contains a Bioengineered Food Ingredient" is the first option and the one that GM labeling advocates wanted to be required (USDA 2019). The other options available to manufacturers are a USDA approved symbol, electronic or digital (scan here) disclosure, and text message disclosure. Producers can choose a disclosure option that meets their marketing needs and is consistent with industry's SmartLabel QR code initiative. AMS approved two label symbols, with color and black and white versions. The overtly promotional smiley suns were rejected, but the approved labels are attractive; they show idealized green field rows, a flowering plant, yellow sun, and blue sky. They are intended as a marketing communication that emphasizes agriculture, that is, more nature than science, clearly not a warning. The images differ only in the words "bioengineered" for the required label and "derived from bioengineering" for the voluntary label on foods that don't meet the definition of Bioengineered foods.

CONCLUSIONS

The food industry and its allies dominated the national legislative discourse. Their narratives focused on a pressing interstate *commerce* problem that required a uniform national solution to protect the system of food production, distribution, and sale, and thereby protect consumers from misinformation and higher prices. Their claims that production costs and consumer prices would rise went largely unchallenged, despite evidence that foods labels changed regularly, and GM foods were already labeled for export. In their narrative phrases and frames, lawmakers showed responsiveness to calls for science-based policy in the public interest. They repeated narratives of innovation and *progress* framing, with bi-partisan consensus that agri-biotechnology reduced environmental resource and global population problems. In this case, commercial values were perceived to coincide with scientific consensus and global health, rather than the tension seen in climate change policy. The environmental coalition and Senate Democrats won a mandatory rather than voluntary disclosure, which shows consumer "right to know' *communication* frames influenced the policy outcome, even as labeling advocates' risk and safety frames were sidelined.

GM labeling advocates tried to limit industry domination of the disclosure standard, shifting to the federal court to challenge a rulemaking delay in 2017 while mobilizing public comments to AMS about the proposed BE rules and labels. They were outmatched by industry lobbying and commercial narratives in BE disclosure development. The new national labeling regime, favoring industry options in disclosing bioengineered foods, represents a shift away from the devolution of power trend in federalism. Federal preemption of states' laws undermined the mandatory labeling movement and raises age-old questions of federal incursion on state police powers to regulate health and welfare. Preemption of hard-won state laws is controversial. The fiercest critics in the fractured pro-labeling coalition charge that preemption at the behest of the food industry undermined democratic state policymaking in the public interest.

The policy shift brought by GM labeling advocates was ultimately muted, and the food policy subsystem has reverted back to an industry-friendly regulatory venue at USDA. Industry averted strict labeling mandates that threatened their commercial interests and won new resources to promote bioengineered food through marketing and consumer education. AMS programs for bioengineered foods might evolve to look like promotions for meat and dairy in nutritional guidelines and school lunch programs. Regulatory deference to industry in production and sale will persist as groups continue to debate whether the final bioengineered foods disclosure rules balance transparency, accuracy, and fairness for consumers, producers, and grocers. Compliance is required by January 1, 2020. AMS can investigate and audit records, but no sanctions are established for noncompliance. Conflicts over disclosure implementation will likely continue and may lead to more venue switching by policy challengers.

REFERENCES

Bailey, Pamela G. "Anti-GMO Cleanup Needed on Aisle 4" *Wall Street Journal,* May 7, 2015.

Baumgartner, Frank R, and Jones, Bryan D. "Agenda Dynamics and Policy Subsystems." *The Journal of Politics* 53, no.4 (1991): 1044–74.

Baumgartner, Frank R, and Jones, Bryan D. *Agendas and Instability in American Politics.* Chicago: University of Chicago Press (1993).

Brasher, Philip. "Roberts, Stabenow Reach Deal on GMO Labeling." *Agripulse,* June 26, 2016.

Brody, Jane E. "Fear, Not Fact, Behind G.M.O. Labeling" *New York Times,* June 8, 2015.

Brüggemann, Michael, and D'Angelo, Paul. "Defragmenting News Framing Research: Reconciling Generic and Issue-Specific Frames." In *Doing News Framing Analysis II,* edited by Paul D'Angelo, 90-111. New York: Routledge (2018).

Cobb, Roger, and Charles Elder. Participation in American Politics: The Dynamics of Agenda-Building. Boston: Allyn and Bacon, Inc (1972).

Consumer Reports Food Safety and Sustainability Center. "Report on GMOs in Corn and Soy." *Greener Choices,* (2014). Accessed 4/17/2019. http://greenerchoices.org/wp-content/uploads/2016/09/CR_FSASC_GMO_Final_Report_10102014.pdf

Deloitte. "Study of Electronic or Digital Link Disclosure: A Third-Party Evaluation of Challenges Impacting Access to Bioengineered Food Disclosure." July 2017. Accessed April 29, 2019. https://www.ams.usda.gov/sites/default/files/media/USDADeloitteStudyofElectronicorDigital Disclosure20170801.pdf

Dibden, Jacqui, David Gibbs, and Chris Cocklin. "Framing GM Crops as a Food Security Solution." *Journal of Rural Studies* 29, no. 2 (2013): 59–70.

Ford, Dana and Lorenzo Ferrigno. "Vermont Governor Signs GMO Food Labeling into Law." *CNN.com,* May 8, 2014. Accessed May 1, 2019. https://www.cnn.com/2014/05/08/health/vermont-gmo-labeling/index.html

Frank, Chris. "Rep. Pompeo: GMO's Safe and Don't Need Labelling." 2015. *KAKE ABC,* Aug. 11. Available at: http://coalitionforsafeaffordablefood.org/news/kake-abc-rep-pompeo-gmos-safe-and-dont-need-labeling/

Gasparro, Annie. "ConAgra Going Nationwide With GMO Labeling; Vermont Law's Requirement Having a Big Effect on Food Companies" *Wall Street Journal,* Mar 22, 2016.

Haddon, Heather. "U.S. Senate Approves Legislation Requiring GMO Labels; GMO label bill to be considered by House." *Wall Street Journal,* July 8, 2016.

Keel, G.L. "Commercial Free Speech Trumps the Politics of Food Labeling: The Legacy of Rbst-Free Milk Mandate and Prohibition Cases for Genetic Engineering Disclosure Laws." *First Amendment Studies* 48, no. 1 (2014): 44–60. doi:10.1080/21689725.2014.888860.

Kelly, Julie. "The March of Genetic Food Progress" *Wall Street Journal,* Dec. 30, 2015.

Kingdon, John W. 1995. *Agendas, Alternatives, and Public Policies.* 2nd ed. New York: Longman.

Kysar, Douglas. 2004. "Preferences for Processes: The Process/Product Distinction and the Regulation of Consumer Choice" *Cornell Law Faculty Publications,* Paper 8. Accessed August 16, 2013. http://scholarship.law.cornell.edu/lsrp_papers/8.

McBeth, Mark K., Elizabeth A. Shanahan, Ruth J. Arnell, Paul L. Hathaway. 2007. "The Intersection of Narrative Policy Analysis and Policy Change Theory." *Policy Studies Journal* 35 (1): 87-108.

Morris, Mary H. "The Political Strategies of Winning and Losing Coalitions." *Policy and Politics* 35, no. 4 (2007): 836-871.

Nelson, T. E. and E. A. Willey. 2001. "Issue Frames that Strike a Value Balance: A Political Psychology Perspective." In *Framing Public Life,* edited by Stephen D Reese, Oscar H Gandy, August E Grant. Mahwah, NJ: Lawrence Erlhbaum.

Pralle, Sarah B. "Agenda Setting and Climate Change." *Environmental Politics* 18, no. 5 (2009): 781-799.

Rochefort, David A., and Roger W.Cobb. 1994. *The Politics of Problem Definition: Shaping the Policy Agenda*. Lawrence, Kan.: University Press of Kansas.

Sabatier, Paul A., and Hank C. Jenkins-Smith. 1993. *Policy Change and Learning: An Advocacy Coalition Approach*. Boulder, Colo.: Westview Press.

State of Ohio. 2008. "Labeling of Dairy Product." Administrative Code §901: 11-8-01 (b) (2).

Steinhauer, Jennifer, and Stephanie Strom. "Senate to Vote on GMO Food Labeling Bill" *New York Times*, Mar. 16, 2016.

Stone, Deborah A. 2012. *Policy Paradox: The Art of Political Decision Making*. Third ed. New York: W.W. Norton & Company.

Sundar, Sindhu. 2015. "Vermont GMO Case Could Shape State Food Labeling Powers" *Law360*. Accessed April 19, 2019. http://www.law360.com/articles/702970/.

Tversky, Amos and Daniel Kahneman. "The Framing of Decisions and the Psychology of Choice." *Science* 211, no. 4481 (1981): 453-458.

U.S. Department of Agriculture. Agriculture Marketing Service. "About AMS" https://www.ams.usda.gov/about-ams. Accessed April 28, 2019.

———. 2018. "Establishment of a National Bioengineered Food Disclosure Standard." Docket ID: AMS-TM-17-0050. *Regulations.gov*. Accessed April 20, 2019. https://www.regulations.gov/docketBrowser?rpp=50&so=ASC&sb=organization&po=250&dct=PS&D=AMS-TM-17-0050.

———. 2019. "Industry Fact Sheet – National Bioengineered Food Disclosure Standard" Accessed April 30, 2019. https://www.ams.usda.gov/resources/industry-fact-sheet-national-bioengineered-food-disclosure-standard.

U.S. Food and Drug Administration. 2015. "FDA Takes Several Actions Involving Genetically Engineered Plants and Animals for Food" FDA press release, Nov. 19. Accessed Oct 2, 2016. http://www.fda.gov/NewsEvents/Newsroom/PressAnnouncements/ucm473249.htm

———. 2019. Guidance for Industry: Voluntary Labeling Indicating Whether Foods Have or Have Not Been Derived from Genetically Engineered Plants. Accessed April 26, 2019. https://www.fda.gov/Food/GuidanceRegulation/Guidance DocumentsRegulatoryInformation/ucm059098.htm.

———. 2001. *Guidance for Industry: Voluntary Labeling Indicating Whether Foods Have or have Not Been Developed Using Bioengineering*. Accessed April 26, 2019. https://www.federalregister.gov/documents/2001/01/18/01-1047/draft-guidance-for-industry-voluntary-labeling-indicating-whether-foods-have-or-have-not-been.

———. 1992. "Statement of Policy: Foods Derived from New Plant Varieties" *Federal Register* 57, no. 104 (May 29, 1992): 22984. Accessed May 1, 2019. https://www.fda.gov/regulatory-information/search-fda-guidance-documents/statement-policy-foods-derived-new-plant-varieties

U.S. House of Representatives. Committee on Agriculture. 2015. "Safe and Accurate Food Labeling Act of 2015" (to accompany H.R. 1599) (H. Rpt. 114-208). Washington: Government Printing Office.

U.S. House of Representatives. Office of Congressman Mike Pompeo. 2016. "Pompeo Applauds Historic Food Labeling Bill Being Signed Into Law." Press release. Aug. 1.

U.S. Senate. Committee on Agriculture, Nutrition & Forestry. 2016a. "Agriculture Biotechnology: A Look at Federal Regulation and Stakeholder Perspectives." (10/21/15) (S. Hrg. 114-261). Washington: Government Printing Office.

———. 2016b. "Section by section for the Chairman's Mark on Biotech Labeling" (3/1/16). Accessed 12/28/18. https://www.agriculture.senate.gov/imo/media/doc/Sec-by-sec%20for%20Chairman's%20Mark.pdf.

U.S. Senate. Committee on Agriculture, Nutrition & Forestry. 2016c. "Senate Agriculture Committee Passes Chairman's Mark on biotechnology Labeling Solutions." (3/1/16). Accessed 12/28/18. https://www.agriculture.senate.gov/newsroom/rep/press/release/senate-agriculture-committee-passes-chairmans-mark-on-biotechnology-labeling-solutions-.

————. 2016d. "A National Bioengineering Labeling Standard" (to accompany S. 2609) (S. Rpt. 114-403). Washington: Government Printing Office.
Wooten, Casey. "GMO Lobbying Spiked 31 Percent in First Quarter." *Bloomberg BNA,* May 9, 2016.

CHAPTER 4

The Future of Fairtrade from Farm to Shelf

Alissa Bilfield (University of Arizona)

INTRODUCTION

Since the first fair trade certification was implemented, 1.6 million farmers and workers have participated in the fair trade system, and global sales have reached 8.95 billion dollars.[1] From its inception in the early 20th century, the fair trade movement was originally inspired to provide a market to small producers and artisans in developing countries. Decades of organizing culminated in the creation of certification systems in the late 1990s with corresponding consumer-facing labels.[2]

Gaining momentum from the movement, the fair trade certification was more radically envisioned to serve as a development mechanism that could begin to address the structural inequalities of modern agriculture within the developing world. Unjust land tenure policies, inhumane working conditions, child labor practices, gender inequality, and poor environmental standards were just a few of the issues that this broad-based standard meant to address through certification. Initially, only small-holder producer organizations, namely agricultural cooperatives, associations, and federations were eligible to certify their commodities as fair trade. Through the certification system these producer organizations have been guaranteed a fair trade minimum price as a protection against the uncertainties of the market economy. In addition, fair trade certification provides producer organizations an annual social premium that is reimbursed to be used to fund democratically determined projects. Social premiums have helped to support projects ranging from community health projects, to education scholarships, to reinvesting back in their production processes.[3,4]

---

[1] Fairtrade International. 2017. Annual Report: Creating Innovations, Scaling Impact. Published online:https://annualreport16-17.fairtrade.net/en/

[2] Laura T. Reynolds, Douglas Murray, and Peter Leigh Taylor, "Fair Trade Coffee: Building Producer Capacity via Global Networks," *Journal of International Development*16, no. 8 (2004): 1109-121, doi:10.1002/jid.1136.

[3] Alex Nicholls and Charlotte Opal, *Fair Trade: Market Driven Ethical Consumption* (London: Sage Publications, 2005).

Now, the fair trade movement has evolved and multiplied, with a growing number of variations in fair trade labeling schemes and certifications utilized globally. Significant research highlights the tangible benefits of fair trade, ranging from improved community health outcomes to gender empowerment to livelihood diversification. Critics have also voiced concern over the comparatively limited improvements for producers, corporate cooption of fair trade, the lack of significant systemic change that the standard originally sought to catalyze, and the weaknesses inherent in a now disjointed system.

This chapter will explore the historical context of the creation of fair trade certification and the evolution of the original standard into the multiple iterations that exist today. The content will also include a description of the current fair trade labeling practices and an analysis of the policies, politics, and power represented by the inclusion of fair trade as a label. Finally, through the lens of small holder farmers and supply chain stakeholders, this chapter will discuss the impacts of the fair trade label with regards to social and environmental impact, marketing, and governance.

HISTORY & CONTEXT

The origins of the modern fair trade movement are inherently linked to the development of the co-operative movement in the late nineteenth century. In its modern form, the fair trade movement can be traced to the late 1940s, where parallel models were developing in the United States and Europe.[5,6] First motivated by individuals, and then by organized groups, individuals involved in the early movement were altruistically motivated and saw an opportunity to provide better markets to artisans and producers working in the developing world. Whereas in the US, the movement's origins can be traced to faith communities such as the Mormons, in Europe fair trade arose to meet the needs of domestic refugees.

The origins of fair trade in the USA are most notably rooted in the story of Edna Ruth Byler, a Mormon entrepreneur who traveled with her husband to Puerto Rico, and observed an opportunity to help women living in poverty trying to support their families by selling their high quality needle-work back in the USA. She once made the self-observation, "I am just a woman, trying to help other women." As the story is recounted, she began the business from the trunk of a car, buying needle work, selling it, and then returning to Puerto Rico to deliver the profits to the women. The business was successful, and launched into a brick and mortar establishment in 1958 called "Self Help Crafts,' which eventually became the

---

[4] Sandro Castaldo, Francesco Perrini, Nicola Misani, and Antonio Tencati, "The Missing Link Between Corporate Social Responsibility and Consumer Trust: The Case of Fair Trade Products," *Journal of Business Ethics* 84, no. 1 (2008): 1-15, doi:10.1007/s10551-0089669-4.
[5] World Fair Trade Organization, *Annual Report 2017*, 2017, https://wfto.com/sites/default/files/WFTO%20Annual%20Report%202017.pdf
[6] Mukhisa Kituyi, "Fifty Years of Promoting Trade and Development," *International Trade Forum* 2014, no. 2 (2014): 28-31, doi:10.18356/db1c4549-en.

highly successful franchise store, Ten Thousand Villages, that now sells both handicrafts and food items including coffee, tea, and grains.[7]

Meanwhile, in Europe, Oxfam began selling fair trade crafts created by Chinese refugees in Oxfam shops in the United Kingdom (UK). In 1964 the first Fair Trade Organization was created by Oxfam, while parallel initiatives were taking place in the Netherlands, the most famous for sugar cane. These first-wave fair trade shops provided a point of sales, but perhaps more importantly they were the first hubs of activity in fair trade campaigning and awareness-raising. In the decades that followed, non-profit organizations across the globe perceived the need for fair trade marketing organizations to support the burgeoning *"trade not aid'* dialogue within the international development community, which resulted in the creation of a variety of Southern Fair Trade Organizations that were linked to newly established fair trade organizations in the global North ,with a goal of creating equity in international trade through partnership, dialogue, transparency, and respect.[8]

Initially referred to as "alternative trade,' the fair trade movement grew in response to poverty and inequity observed in the global South with a goal of providing not just a market for producers, but also social services to politically and economically marginalized communities. Although the initial origins of the formal certification were relatively disparate, they coalesced into fair trade certification over the course of a decade between the 1980s and 1990s when coffee was integrated into the movement. Formal certification in Europe began first, with coffee and the private label Max Havallar in 1988, and almost a decade later Transfair was created in the USA in 1998. These independent labeling organizations set the standards for fair trade certification, and in 1997 an umbrella organization, Fairtrade International, was established to coordinate the various definitions of fair trade across national borders. The efforts of these organizations provided legitimacy to the fair trade label and helped to propel the movement and spread of fair trade throughout the 1990s and early 2000s.

During this period, fair trade grew into a heterogeneous movement "composed of overlapping networks and coalitions of activists and NGOs."[9] While the labeling standards have evolved, the main focus has been on providing a niche specialty market to small farmers and producers in an effort to assuage the inequities in the global agricultural market while building democratically enhanced community resilience. Up to this point, the main focus of fair trade had been on supporting small-holder producer cooperative organizations. These producer organizations would receive the fair trade minimum price for their products, and in addition they would also receive an annual social premium reimbursement that the cooperative could reinvest into their community. This could take the form of additional

[7] "History of 10,000 Villages," Ten Thousand Villlages, 2018, https://www.tenthousandvillages.com/about-history.
[8] "History of Fair Trade," World Fair Trade Organization, 2018, https://wfto.com/about-us/history-wfto/history-fair-trade.
[9] Frederick H. Buttel and Kenneth A. Gould, "Global Social Movement(s) at the Crossroads: Some Observations on the Trajectory of the Anti-Corporate Globalization Movement," *Journal of World-Systems Research* 10, no. 1 (2004): 37-66, doi:10.5195/jwsr.2004.309.

technical assistance, establishing small-scale agricultural facilities, developing an education scholarship fund for cooperative school children, or other projects focused on health, nutrition, or gender equity. The most important aspect of the premium was that the democratically organized cooperative associations would decide how to use the funds.

DEFINITION

While the history of this movement has and will continue to evolve, a widely accepted definition of fair trade is as follows:

> *Fair trade is a trading partnership, based on dialogue, transparency, and respect, which seeks greater equity in international trade. It contributes to sustainable development by offering better trading conditions to, and securing the rights of, marginalized producers and workers – especially in the South. Fair trade organizations (backed by consumers) are engaged actively in supporting producers, awareness raising, and in campaigning for changes in the rules and practice of conventional international trade.*[10]

From this definition, the broad-based goals of fair trade include:

1. To improve the livelihoods and well-being of producers by improving market access, strengthening producer organizations, paying a better price and providing continuity in the trading relationship.
2. To promote development opportunities for disadvantaged producers, especially women and indigenous people, and to protect children from exploitation in the production process.
3. To raise awareness among consumers of the negative effects on producers of fair trade so that they exercise their purchasing power positively
4. To set an example of partnership in trade through dialogue, transparency, and respect.
5. To campaign for changes in the rules and practice of conventional international trade.
6. To protect human rights by promoting social justice, sound environmental practices, and economic security.[11]

INDUSTRY STRUCTURE, LABELING POLICIES, AND PROCESSES

The organizations that are a part of the fair trade movement include producer organizations, buying organizations, umbrella bodies that bring together both

---

[10] "Definition of Fair Trade," World Fair Trade Organization, 2019, https://wfto.com/fair-trade/definition-fair-trade.

[11] Andy Redfern and Paul Snedker, "Creating Market Opportunities for Small Enterprises: Experiences of the Fair Trade Movement" (Geneva: ILO, 2002).

producers and buyers, and retail organizations. Whereas consumers may just see a label on a package, behind the label lies a complex multi-tiered system of standards, auditing protocols, monitoring and evaluation, and assessment. Standard setting is part of one of the major industry structures of the fair trade movement. There are two original standard setting agencies: the International Federation of Alternative Trade (IFAT) and Fairtrade Labeling Organizations International (FLO). IFAT, which is now referred to as the World Fair Trade Organization (WFTO), traditionally worked with craft producers, who have sold their product through the alternative trade channels. These standards are continually updated and operate on a biennial self-assessment basis and cover:

- Creating opportunities for economically disadvantaged producers;
- Transparency and accountability
- Capacity building
- Promoting Fair Trade
- Payment of a fair price
- Gender equity
- Working conditions
- Child Labor
- The environment.

The FLO standards operate differently: as opposed to the WFTO, which focuses more on organizational certification, FLO standards focus on product-based certification. In both contexts, these standards continue to evolve, and almost every year changes are made to the requirements of the certification process to enhance and improve upon the system. Once organizations at various levels of the supply chain are certified, they must comply with the standards as they are upgraded. This section will first provide an overview of the complex certification standards at the core of Fairtrade International's process, followed by a summary of the other major fair trade certifications that exist.

At the core of Fairtrade International's continued standards is that in order for a product to be certified, it must be produced by small farmers who are part of a cooperative organization. In addition, only producers from specified countries can be included in the geographic scope of the label. Considerations regarding income per capita, wealth disparities, and other economic and social indicators are taken into account, as well as the long-term impact for producers. Based on these national-level standards, members of the European Union and G8 countries are excluded. Individual farmers are considered to be small producers if they meet certain set standards based on the crops that they grow. For example, farmers growing less intensive crops such as cacao, coffee, herbs, spices, honey, and nuts are considered to be "small producers' if they meet the following requirements:

- Farm work is mostly done by members and their families.
- They do not hire workers all year round, unless they are producing highly labor-intensive products (cane sugar, prepared

and preserved fruit & vegetables, fresh fruit, fresh vegetables, tea).

- They hire less than a maximum number of permanent workers, as defined and published by Fairtrade International.
- The size of the land they cultivate is equal to or below the average of the region, as defined and published by Fairtrade International.
- They spend most of their working time doing agricultural work on their farm.
- Most of their income comes from their farm.

Producer organizations can be rated as 1st grade, 2nd grade, and 3rd grade. For example, a cooperative organization comprised directly of small farmers as legal members would be rated as a 1st grade producer organization, whereas a 2nd grade producer organization may be a federation that unites multiple cooperative organizations made up of small farmers. A 3rd grade organization would unite 2nd grade member organizations: at each grading, the entity is further removed from the core of small producers. For producers, there are a set of core standards that must be met to qualify as a fair trade producer once you are a member of a 1st grade organization, and then added development requirements that demonstrate a commitment to continuous improvement that must also be undertaken annually. Certified producer organizations are rated based on a points system, where they get credit for complying and continuing to develop and improve in different areas. Each of the core requirements is audited annually, every three years, or every six years, depending.

There are extensive protocols for fair trade certified producer organizations that have been outlined in detail. The table below provides an overview of the three main categories, each of which contain within them multiple subcategories.[12]

Table 1: Major Categories of Protocols for Fair Trade Certified Producer Organizations

Trade	Traceability, sourcing, contracts, use of fair trade mark
Production	Management, environmental development, soil and water, waste, genetically modified organizations, biodiversity, energy and greenhouse gas emissions, labor conditions, freedom of association and collective bargaining, occupational health and safety
Business Development	Development potential, democracy/participation, transparency, non-discrimination

TRADERS

Fairtrade traders are also required to be certified in order to establish a mutually beneficial and sustained trade relationship and to provide greater transparency. Just as producers have to meet core requirements with added development standards, so,

---

[12] "Fairtrade Standards for Small-scale Producer Organizations," Fairtrade International, 2019, https://www.fairtrade.net/fileadmin/user_upload/content/2009/standards/SPO_EN.pdf.

too, do traders. Traders are considered all who buy, sell, or process fair trade certified products, up to the point where the product is in its final packaging. This may take different forms depending on the products and their supply chains. For fruit, a crop that may have a shorter supply chain, producers often label and package the product at their own site, which would mean the producers are certified as both producers and traders. In the coffee value chain, a 2nd grade coffee federation that unites multiple cooperatives may be considered to be a trader, in addition to a roaster that imports green coffee beans and then packages and sells them to retailers. Traders who want to become certified must comply with protocols outlined in detail in the standards guide for traders.[13] The table below provides an overview of the three main categories, each of which contain within them various subcategories.

Table 2: Major Categories of Protocols for Fair Trade Certified Traders

Trade	Traceability, mass balance, product composition
Generic Requirements	Right to trade, use of the fair trade mark
Production	Labor, environment
Business Development	Contracts, fair trade price and premium, price levels, timely payment, access to finance, sourcing plan and market information, sharing risks, capacity building, trading with integrity

These standards apply to all traders who buy and sell fair trade products or handle the fair trade price and premium. The main components of fair and sustainable trading focus on ensuring that traders uphold the central mechanisms of fair trade. Broadly speaking, these include transparency of transactions, giving producers at least the fair trade minimum price in addition to the fair trade premium, working collaboratively on sourcing plans, supporting access to pre-finance so that producers can fund their operations, and trading with integrity.

PRICING

Pricing is determined through producer data collected by fair trade that estimates production costs. Fair trade maintains data on the Cost of Sustainable Production (COSP), which is one of the key sources of information that informs the development of Fairtrade Minimum Prices. Fairtrade Minimum Prices (FMP) are aimed at protecting producers from market instabilities, providing a safety net in case of low prices. COSP data is crucial. In addition to Fairtrade minimum prices, producer organizations also receive a Fairtrade Premium.

LABELING STANDARDS

The proliferation of a variety of fair trade standards adopted by different organizations under different labels represents both differing philosophical and

---

[13] "Fairtrade Standards for Small-scale Producer Organizations," Fairtrade International, 2019, https://www.fairtrade.net/fileadmin/user_upload/content/2009/standards/SPO_EN.pdf.

logical practices, in addition to opportunity recognition on behalf of certifying organizations. In 2012, the movement confronted the largest divide to date, when Fairtrade USA became an independent organization and implemented a new policy called *"Fair Trade for All"*, which included more types of farms including large-scale plantations into its certification system. Up until this point, while there were differences among the various labeling organizations that had been established, the underlying similarity was that to be certified, the producer organization had to be considered a small-holder organization comprised of small-holder producers. This divide continues to shape the dialogue of power and politics in the fair trade movement amongst the growing number of certification programs and labels. While there are a variety of labeling programs that have integrated fair trade concepts into their protocols, the following half dozen labels represent the most popular that directly focus on fair trade.

Table 3: Overview of Major Labeling Program for Fair Trade Products

	Fairtrade International Also known as the Fairtrade Labeling Organization (FLO), Fairtrade International is the leading labeling organization in the United States today. Based in Germany, FLO has both a certifying branch and a standard-setting branch.
	Fairtrade USA A non-profit third-party certifier of fair trade products in North America. Fair Trade USA audits and certifies transactions between domestic companies and international suppliers to ensure that farmers and workers are paid fair prices and wages, work in safe conditions, protect the environment, and receive community development funds to empower and improve their communities. Previously called TransFair USA, it was a member of FLO but split from the organization in 2011 to allow multinational corporations running plantation-style agriculture to use their fair trade logo.
	Fair for Life Created by the Swiss Bio Foundation, the Institute for Market ecology (IMO) and Social & Fair Trade Certification has developed the Fair for Life label. This label is focused on human rights at any stage of production, and that smallholder farmers receive a fair share. Fair for life is a brand neutral third-party certification program. It does not use product-specific standards.

	Equal Exchange Equal Exchange was founded in 1986 as one of the original alternative trade organizations that helped to catalyze the modern fair trade movement in the United States. A for-profit company, Equal Exchange maintains an alternative trade model that utilizes direct trade, established long term contracts, and offers higher-than-market prices to small coffee farmers. The company remains committed to supporting small farmers and producer organizations.
	Whole Trade Whole Foods, a large grocery retailer, uses a "white label" for their own stores called Whole Trade. They rely on third-party certifiers including Fair Trade USA, Rainforest Alliance, Fair for Life, and Fairtrade International. Products are co-labeled – for example a Fair for Life certified banana sold at Whole Foods will also have the Whole Trade Guarantee label.
	Direct Trade As an alternative to Fair Trade, Direct Trade is a model that does not use third party certification. It is most commonly used in the specialty coffee industry and grew out of concerns that Fair Trade was difficult to access, that is, too strict or costly for some producers or retailers. It allows for individual purchasers to be more flexible and more true to their values and goals by buying the product directly from producers. In some cases, it allows for the producer to receive higher compensation than under Fair Trade.

THE POLITICS OF PROLIFERATION

As mentioned previously, between 2011 and 2012 Fairtrade International officially split, and a separate organization, Fairtrade USA emerged with divergent standards. This split was emblematic of pre-existing issues within the fair trade movement that had already led to the establishment of a number of different fair trade labels, all with their own varied approach to supporting their vision of fair trade through certification. The rift within Fairtrade international occurred over a philosophical difference regarding who should be certified. Whereas Fairtrade International wanted to continue to only certify small-holder organizations, Fairtrade USA was open to certifying plantation-scale operations, supporting a new philosophy they branded as *"Fair Trade for All."* Both organizations maintain a commitment to the original standards that have been established, but Fairtrade USA's work now extends into also certifying larger farms that rely on wage labor for production and harvesting. On one hand, Fairtrade International saw fair trade as a mechanism for providing market access to small-holder farmers in developing countries. On the other hand, Fairtrade USA saw that while supporting small-holder farmers is an important mission, an even larger number of agricultural wage workers remained unprotected that could benefit from the support of fair trade. This difference of approach caused a fundamental bifurcation of the fair trade movement. The global group viewed the inclusion of large-scale commercial farms as incompatible with the core values and goals of fair trade, which has been to support and provide a market for small-holder farmers.

Fairtrade USA cited three major reasons for the shift to "Fair Trade for All." The first was to reduce inconsistencies that already existed in the certification of plantation-grown products such as bananas and tea that had been eligible for the certification process. The move to include coffee was arguably the most controversial, since plantation-grown coffee had been excluded up until this point. Another argument was that by expanding the fair trade market, a greater number of farmers and farm-workers would benefit, by improved labor laws, access to healthcare, and improved living conditions. There were also sentiments that fair trade was just scratching the surface of inequity in the agricultural labor market, and that by opening up the certification to cover agricultural wage workers, whether they were working on plantations or on small-holder land, more expansive humanitarian improvements could be gained.

Concerns over this shift remain. On a practical level, it can be difficult for consumers, and even retailers and producers, to distinguish between different labels. While emerging research will continue to shed light on the implications of the proliferation of fair trade certification labels, it has been forecasted by some critics that the current situation has weakened existing standards, undermined their legitimacy, and established competing standards.[14] Ultimately the divisions in the fair trade movement represent a fundamental debate over the purpose of fair trade. Scholars question if the central purpose to leverage social and environmental justice for small producers by creating a niche market for their products through certification. Or is it meant to address social and environmental issues at scale throughout all levels of agribusiness? Perhaps even more concerning are the implications related to power and governance. Farmers, who are supposed to be at the center of concern, have not been included in the decision-making process at fair trade USA.[15]

Either way, the current fragmentation of the fair trade movement, which is now spread over a growing number of organizations and certifying bodies with their own corresponding labels, has created a more confusing marketplace. At the same time,

---

[14] Maki Hatanaka, Jason Konefal, and Douglas H. Constance, "A Tripartite Standards Regime Analysis of the Contested Development of a Sustainable Agriculture Standard," *Agriculture and HumanValues* 29, no. 1 (2011): 65-78 doi:10.1007/s10460-011-9329-7.

[15] Daniel Jaffee and Philip H. Howard, "Who's the Fairest of Them All? The Fractured Landscape of U.S. Fair Trade Certification," *Agriculture and Human Values* 33, no. 4 (2015): 813-26, doi:10.1007/s10460-015-9663-2

consumers, retailers, and producers who scratch below the surface of the label may be inclined to support more rigorous seals, which could lead to positive competition. In the best-case scenario, the rifts between the labels may in the end promote a strengthening of the system overall, whereby the movement is able to evolve through the mechanism of "fighting standards with standards.'[16]

DISCOURSES OF POLITICS AND POWER

One of the original goals of fair trade has been to challenge international norms related to free trade. To achieve this goal, fair trade organizations have had to operate both "in' and "against' the market.[17] As such, there have been inevitable tensions. Is fair trade fair? Critics have questioned whether fair trade could ever be authentically anti-hegemonic, since it operates within the confines of market structures and does not challenge the ideology of consumerism.[18] Furthermore, critics also point out further constraints to the system that supports lingering power asymmetry between the global North and the global South, a conservative understanding of empowerment by the movement, limited participation of southern partners, and the unequal distribution of responsibilities along the fair trade commodity chain.[19,20] Three main discourses exist outlined in an analysis by Low and Davenport in 2006 that explore the politics and power of fair trade. These include:

> **Adoption:** While adoption of fair trade is far from being widespread, the discourse of adoption within the fair trade movement suggests that alternative channels for fair trade should not be necessary. Rather, these standards should be embedded into the standards of all businesses. The false pretense of providing a consumer choice between "exploitative' bananas and Fairtrade bananas would no longer be an accepted norm.[21]

> **Assimilation:** In assimilation, fair trade would be integrated into mainstream commercial trade, but it would remain a small, lucrative niche.

[16] Tad Mutersbaugh, "Fighting Standards with Standards: Harmonization, Rents, and Social Accountability in Certified Agrofood Networks," *Environment and Planning A: Economy and Space* 37, no. 11 (2005): 2033-051, doi:10.1068/a37369.
[17] Laura T. Raynolds, "Consumer/Producer Links in Fair Trade Coffee Networks," *Sociologia Ruralis* 42, no. 4 (2002): 404-24, doi:10.1111/1467-9523.00224.
[18] Josee Johnston, "Consuming Global Justice: Fair Trade shopping and alternative development," in: *Protest and Globalization: Prospects for Transnational Solidarity*, edited by James Goodman (Australia: Pluto Press, 2002).
[19] Linsday Naylor, "Some Are More Fair than Others: Fair Trade Certification, Development, and North South Subjects," *Agriculture and Human Values* 31, no. 2 (2013): 273-84, doi:10.1007/s10460 013-9476-0.
[20] Aimee Shreck, "Resistance, Redistribution, and Power in the Fair Trade Banana Initiative," *Agriculture and Human Values* 22, no. 1 (2005): 17-29, doi:10.1007/s10460 004-7227-y.
[21] Will Low and Davenport, Eileen, "Mainstreaming fair trade: adoption, assimilation, appropriation," *Journal of Strategic Marketing* 14 (2007): 315-327.

This has largely been the case, where fair trade, like organic, has become a segmented product.

Appropriation: Mainstream companies are increasingly using the consumers relatively weak understanding of the fair trade message to their own advantage—'clean washing' or 'image laundering.' Mainstream business appropriating part of the fair trade message while washing that message clean shifts the message from the exploitative nature of trade to the conventional problem of demand and supply.

Ultimately, while there has been a significant body of literature that has criticized fair trade, there is still compelling research that has shown that these systems of certification have made changes in the lives of producers.[22,23,24,25] The next section of this chapter will present major findings from research that has explored the perspectives of fair trade producers themselves.

FAIR TRADE FROM THE PRODUCER PERSPECTIVE

Since the whole fair trade movement has been built around concern for inequitable structural constraints for small farmers and producers in mostly developing countries, it is important to consider their perspectives and experiences around the certification system. To date, a small body of research has directly considered the farmers' perspectives on fair trade. While in some cases farmers are aware of the technical structures of fair trade, others are more well-informed about the broader implications of the system. When asked about their perspectives on fair trade, farmers commonly cite that while the minimum price guarantee is not a panacea, it is more than what they might receive otherwise from local third-party buyers. In addition, farmers appreciate the creation of a more just system: while it is clearly not utopic, it is incrementally better than before. Many farmers also cite the benefits that they have received as members of fair trade cooperatives. It is through these cooperative organizations that farmers benefit from the fair trade price, the social premiums, and the technical and financial assistance programs.

Farmers have voiced that they greatly value the assistance provided to them through the cooperative structure. It is difficult to disentangle the benefits of fair trade from the benefits of membership in a cooperative, but it is clear that the combined effect of cooperative associations implementing fair trade principles

---

[22] Christopher M. Bacon, V. Ernesto Méndez, and Jonathan A. Fox, "Cultivating Sustainable Coffee: Persistent Paradoxes," in *Confronting the Coffee Crisis*, ed. Christopher M. Bacon, et. al. (Cambridge, MA: MIT Press, 2008), 337-72, doi:10.7551/mitpress/9780262026338.003.0014.
[23] Daniel Jaffee, Brewing Justice: Fair Trade Coffee, Sustainability and Survival (Berkeley, CA: University of California Press, 2007).
[24] Sarah Lyon, Josefina Aranda Bezaury, and Tad Mutersbaugh, "Gender Equity in Fairtrade organic Coffee Producer Organizations: Cases from Mesoamerica," *Geoforum* 41, no. 1(2010): 93-103, doi:10.1016/j.geoforum.2009.04.006.
[25] Loraine Ronchi, "The impact of fair trade on producers and their organizations: A case study with Coocafe in Costa Rica" (University of Sussex, UK: Policy Research Unit, 2002).

improves the financial security, education, health, and the opportunity of small producer members.[26]

Broadly categorized, the benefits for producers cited in the literature have included:

- Increased price per pound for farmers
- Benefits of social premium projects
- Access to finances
- Technical assistance
- Opportunities for diversification
- Learning new skills
- Social connection to fellow producers
- Increases individual family incomes
- Improvement in nutrition, health, and education.[27,28,29,30]

Unsurprisingly, the implications of the fair trade market opening to larger plantation-style farms has been of concern for small farmers and their cooperative associations. Since the split in 2012 between Fairtrade International and Fairtrade USA, there has been strong opposition from small producer organizations for expanding plantation certification to crops that have previously banned such a practice.[31] Relatedly, one of the most serious issues now facing fair trade producers is that in some years the supply currently outpaces the demand. Some research has estimated that 20 percent of the global supply of fair trade certified coffee is actually sold at the fair trade minimum price. Across all products, it is estimated that only 31% of these organizations' harvests were sold at fair trade terms in 2011. As a result, many farmers work hard to meet fair trade certification's standards, but sell their crops at the lower prices set on the commodities market.[32,32] Qualitative research also supports these statistics, as farmers have divulged that sometimes all of their crop cannot be sold at the fair trade established rate.

---

[26] Alex Nicholls and Benjamin Huybrechts, "Fair Trade and Co-operatives," *Oxford Handbooks Online* (2017) doi:10.1093/oxfordhb/9780199684977.013.33.

[27] Leonardo Becchetti and Marco Costantino, "The Effects of Fair Trade on Affiliated Producers: An Impact Analysis on Kenyan Farmers," *World Development* 36, no. 5 (2008): 823-42, doi:10.1016/j.worlddev.2007.05.007.

[28] Bob Doherty and Sophi Tranchell, "New Thinking in International Trade? A Case Study of The Day Chocolate Company," *Sustainable Development* 13, no. 3 (2005): 166-76, doi:10.1002/sd.273.

[29] Laura Raynolds, "Poverty Alleviation through Participation in Fair Trade Coffee Cooperatives: Existing Research and Critical Issues," (Fort Collins, CO: University of Colorado Press, 2002).

[30] Alastair Smith, "The Fair Trade Cup is Two-thirds Full, not Two-thirds Empty," ESRC Research Centre: Business, Relationships, Accountability, Sustainability, and Society, University of Cardiff (2008).

[31] Renard and Loconto, "Competing logics in the further standardization of fair trade: ISEAL and the Simbolo de Pequencos Productores, *International Journal of Sociology of Agriculture and Food* 20, no. 1 (2013): 51-68.

[32] "Monitoring the Scope and Benefits of Fairtrade, 4th edition" Fairtrade International, (2012).

FOR THE FUTURE

As the fair trade movement continues to evolve, more research and market-based analysis will emerge to distill the impacts of recent changes to the system. While these challenges are important to acknowledge, the benefits of fair trade and participation in cooperative associations for small producers should not be underestimated. Rather, what is needed now is a focus on systemic change, first at the level of the fair trade movement. Interestingly, as a reaction to shifts and changes in the fair trade movement, a growing number of fourth-wave coffee roasters and retailers have started to focus on moving to what they see beyond fair trade to offer what they refer to as "direct trade.' Without a formal third-party verification system like many fair trade labels, this approach relies on the transparency of the business relationships and shortened supply chains that connect retailers directly to producer organizations. Dissatisfied with the complexity and evolution of the fair trade movement, these new models continue to challenge the established fair trade system. Looking to the future, the overarching trends of both fair trade and the move towards direct trade highlight that there is an increased desire for greater transparency and fairness throughout the supply chain, from the producer to the consumer. While current policies, structures, and labeling practices are complex and arguably support very different visions for fair trade, with continued progress and transformation they can continue to meet the original charge of the movement, to improve livelihoods, promote development, raise awareness, enhance trade transparency, and protect human rights by promoting social justice, sound environmental practices, and economic security.

REFERENCES

Bacon, Christopher M., V. Ernesto Méndez, and Jonathan A. Fox. "Cultivating Sustainable Coffee: Persistent Paradoxes." *Confronting the Coffee Crisis*, (2008): 337-72. doi:10.7551/mitpress/9780262026338.003.0014.

Becchetti, Leonardo, and Marco Costantino. "The Effects of Fair Trade on Affiliated Producers: An Impact Analysis on Kenyan Farmers." *World Development*36, no. 5 (2008): 823-842. doi:10.1016/j.worlddev.2007.05.007.

Castaldo, Sandro, Francesco Perrini, Nicola Misani, and Antonio Tencati. "The Missing Link Between Corporate Social Responsibility and Consumer Trust: The Case of Fair Trade Products." *Journal of Business Ethics*84, no. 1 (2008): 1-15. doi:10.1007/s10551-0089669-4.

Cole, Nicki Lisa, and Keith Brown. "The Problem with Fair Trade Coffee." *Contexts* 13, no. 1 (2014):50-55. doi:10.1177/1536504214522009.

Doherty, Bob, and Sophi Tranchell. "New Thinking in International Trade? A Case Study of The Day Chocolate Company." *Sustainable Development*13, no. 3 (2005): 166-76. doi:10.1002/sd.273.

Fairtrade International. "Fairtrade Standards for Small-scale Producer Organizations." 2019. Accessed online: https://www.fairtrade.net/fileadmin/user_upload/content/2009/standards/SPO_EN.pdf

———. 2017. Annual Report: Creating Innovations, Scaling Impact. Published online: https://annualreport16-17.fairtrade.net/en/

———. "Fairtrade Trader Standards." (2015). Accessed online: Fairtrade International. "Fairtrade Standards for Small-scale Producer Organizations." (2019). Accessed online: https://www.fairtrade.net/fileadmin/user_upload/content/2009/standards/SPO_EN.pdf

———. "Monitoring the scope and benefits of fairtrade." (2012). 4th edition. Bonn, Fairtrade International.

Fischer, Edward F., and Bart Victor. "High-End Coffee and Smallholding Growers in Guatemala." *Latin American Research Review*49, no. 1 (2014): 155-77. doi:10.1353/lar.2014.0001.

Hatanaka, Maki, Jason Konefal, and Douglas H. Constance. "A Tripartite Standards Regime Analysis of the Contested Development of a Sustainable Agriculture Standard." *Agriculture and Human Values* 29, no. 1 (2011): 65-78. doi:10.1007/s10460-011-9329-7.

Jaffee, Daniel. Brewing Justice: Fair Trade Coffee, Sustainability and Survival. (2007). University of California Press.

Jaffee, Daniel, and Philip H. Howard. "Corporate Cooptation of Organic and Fair Trade Standards." *Agriculture and Human Values*27, no. 4 (2009): 387-99. doi:10.1007/s10460 009 9231-8.

Jaffee, Daniel, and Philip H. Howard. "Who's the Fairest of Them All? The Fractured Landscape of U.S. Fair Trade Certification." *Agriculture and Human Values*33, no. 4 (2015): 81326. doi:10.1007/s10460-015-9663-2.

Johnston, Josee. "Consuming Global Justice: Fair Trade shopping and alternative development." In: Protest and Globalization: Prospects for Transnational Solidarity (2002). Sydney: Pluto Press Australia.

Kituyi, Mukhisa. "Fifty Years of Promoting Trade and Development." *International Trade Forum* 2014, no. 2 (2014): 28-31. doi:10.18356/db1c4549-en.

Low, Will and Davenport, Eileen. "Mainstreaming fair trade: adoption, assimilation, appropriation." Journal of Strategic Marketing 14, (2007): 315-327.

Lyon, Sarah. "Maya Coffee Farmers and Fair Trade: Assessing the Benefits and Limitations of Alternative Markets." *Culture & Agriculture* 29, no. 2 (2007): 100-12. doi:10.1525/cag.2007.29.2.100.

Lyon, Sarah, Josefina Aranda Bezaury, and Tad Mutersbaugh. "Gender Equity in Fairtrade organic Coffee Producer Organizations: Cases from Mesoamerica." *Geoforum* 41, no. 1 (2010): 93-103. doi:10.1016/j.geoforum.2009.04.006.

Moore, Geoff. "The Fair Trade Movement: Parameters, Issues and Future Research." *Journal of Business Ethics*53, no. 1&2 (2004): 73-86. doi:10.1023/b:busi.0000039400.57827.c3.

Mutersbaugh, Tad. "Fighting Standards with Standards: Harmonization, Rents, and Social Accountability in Certified Agrofood Networks." *Environment and Planning A: Economy and Space* 37, no. 11 (2005): 2033-051. doi:10.1068/a37369.

Naylor, Lindsay. "'Some Are More Fair than Others': Fair Trade Certification, Development, and North South Subjects." *Agriculture and Human Values*31, no. 2 (2013): 273-84. doi:10.1007/s10460 013-9476-0.

Nicholls, Alex, and Benjamin Huybrechts. "Fair Trade and Co-operatives." *Oxford Handbooks Online*, 2017. doi:10.1093/oxfordhb/9780199684977.013.33.

Nicholls, Alex and Opal, Charlotte. Fair Trade: market driven ethical consumption. (2005). Sage Publications, London.

Raynolds, Laura T., Douglas Murray, and Peter Leigh Taylor. "Fair Trade Coffee: Building Producer Capacity via Global Networks." *Journal of International Development* 16, no. 8 (2004): 1109-121. doi:10.1002/jid.1136.

Raynolds, Laura T. "Consumer/Producer Links in Fair Trade Coffee Networks." *Sociologia Ruralis* 42, no. 4 (2002): 404-24. doi:10.1111/1467-9523.00224.

———. "Poverty Alleviation through Participation in Fair Trade Coffee Cooperatives: Existing Research and Critical Issues." (2002). Fort Collins, CO: Colorado State UniversityPress.

Redfern and Snedker. "Creating Market Opportunities for Small Enterprises: Experiences of the Fair Trade Movement." (2002). ILO, Geneva.

Renard and Loconto. "Competing logics in the further standardization of fair trade: ISEAL and the Simbolo de Pequencos Productores. (2013). International Journal of Sociology of Agriculture and Food 20(1): 51-68.

Ronchi, Loraine. "The impact of fair trade on producers and their organizations: A case study with Coocafe in Costa Rica." (2002). Policy Research Unit, University of Sussex, UK.

Smith, Alastair M. "Evaluating The Criticisms Of Fair Trade1." *Economic Affairs* 29, no. 4 (2009): 29-36. doi:10.1111/j.1468-0270.2009.01944.x.

———. "The Fair Trade Cup is Two-thirds Full, not Two-thirds Empty.(2008). ESRC Research Centre: Business, Relationships, Accountability, Sustainability, and Society. University of Cardiff.

Shreck, Aimee. "Resistance, Redistribution, and Power in the Fair Trade Banana Initiative." *Agriculture and Human Values* 22, no. 1 (2005): 17-29. doi:10.1007/s10460 004-7227-y.

Ten Thousand Villlages. "History of 10,000 Villages" (2018). Accessed online: https://www.tenthousandvillages.com/abouthistory/

World Fair Trade Organization. Annual Report 2017. (2017). Accessed online: https://wfto.com/sites/default/files/WFTO%20Annual%20Report%202017.pdf

———. History of Fair Trade. (2018). Accessed online: https://wfto.com/about us/history-wfto/history-fair-trade

———. Definition of Fair Trade. (2019). https://wfto.com/fair-trade/definition-fair-trade

CHAPTER 5

Chicken and Eggs: Cage Free, Free-Range and Pasture Raised

Julia L. Lapp (Ithaca College)

INTRODUCTION

Food labeling practices in the United States have historically focused on the nutritional quality, freshness and wholesomeness of foods. But over the past two decades, with growing concern among consumers about the ethical and ecological issues inherent to the industrialized food system, food labels have increasingly communicated information about these attributes as well. This food labeling practice is referred to as "process labeling," and includes label claims pertaining to an array of practices and processes involved in the production of food that have implications for animal welfare, social justice, and environmental stewardship (Messer, Costanigro, Kaiser, 2017).

Of these process labels, there is a group that is now widely used to describe practices in the production of poultry and eggs. Among these claims are three that describe the living environments or confinement systems in which meat and egg laying poultry are raised. These label claims are "cage free," "free range," and "pasture raised." The living conditions that these labels describe carry multiple implications for the health and welfare of the animals, and, to many, is also indicative of the wholesomeness of the meat or eggs that consumers purchase (Bray & Ankeny, 2017).

This chapter first provides a brief historic background of chicken and egg production practices in the U.S. leading up to the advent of the use of *battery or barren cage* confinement systems used primarily for egg-laying hens, that raises questions related to animal welfare. Next, commonly used systems of confinement that relate to the label terms "cage free," "free range," and "pasture raised" will be discussed in terms of what they are, what incentives for use they provide producers, and the health and welfare implications for animals. Finally, the regulation and oversight of these label claims will be explained.

MEAT AND EGG CHICKEN PRODUCTION IN THE U.S.: A BRIEF HISTORY

Like other commercial agricultural sectors in the U.S., chicken production, for both meat and eggs, has experienced significant transformations over the past century

(McKenna, 2017). The number of overall farms dotting the U.S. landscape has declined from around six million in the early 20th century, to approximately 2 million today (Lyson, 2012). Farms of the past were smaller and more diversified, both in terms of single farms producing a variety of goods and with regard to reliance on a larger array of genetic strains of animals and plants.

Prior to the 1930s, chicken was not a meat staple of U.S. households as beef and pork were (McKenna, 2017). And though chicken was eaten, most chickens were raised on small farms primarily for their eggs, providing an ongoing source of protein without sacrificing the animal. Chicken for meat was secondary. With increased demand and production of eggs during wartime rationing, more young male chickens were sold as "broilers" for meat. (USPEA, 2019; Clauer, 2012). Some chickens were also bred specifically for meat production, but more often, it was the young males and spent or non-productive hens that would be slaughtered for meat. Early 20th century chicken farming relied on dozens of different breeds of chicken that were often specifically bred for hardiness to local environments (Leenstra, Ten Napel, Visscher, Van Sambeek, 2016). Flocks were kept small (up to 200 birds), and egg production per chicken was lower than today's industry standards, averaging 150-200 eggs per year compared with today's average of 250 to 300 eggs (Clauer, 2012).

Chicken production for meat was intentionally developed as food industrialists of the 1940s and 1950s saw a market opportunity for a cheaper alternative to beef and pork. Privations of beef and pork during the war had already increased demand for broiler chickens to some extent. Between 1946 and 1948, under the direction of the United States Department of Agriculture (USDA) and in partnership with national food businesses (such as A&P grocers) as well as land grant colleges and agriculture experiment stations, the "Chicken of Tomorrow" contest set out to encourage producers across the country to develop meat birds that were meatier, tastier, and lower cost as a market competitor to beef or pork (McKenna, 2017). One result of this contest was a shift toward breeding animals that were specifically "designed" for either high meat production or egg production, rather than bred for hardiness to local outdoor environments. Meat hybrids were developed that grew to slaughter weight faster and with higher percentage of lean tissue per bird. As a result, the extensive array of locally bred, pure line breeds of chickens, such as the White Leghorn, Australothorp, Sussex, Plymouth Rock and many others of the early 20th century, rapidly reduced to reliance on just a few hybrids, with most commercial meat hens now being the fast growing Cornish Cross hybrid and the vast majority of commercial egg layers now being only three breeds: New Hampshire Reds, Barred Plymouth Rocks, and White Leghorns (McKenna, 2017; Leenstra, et. al., 2016). Over the decades, with increased commercial production, as genetic variety of birds decreased, flock sizes grew, resulting in rising rates of microbial and parasitic infections. Confinement methods for birds, along with feeding and breeding strategies, became a primary mechanism to continue high levels of meat and egg production while balancing health and unintended mortality risks to birds.

Before the 1950s, all chickens were kept in what today would be considered "free range" or "pasture raised" housing, meaning no cages, where birds were free to roam in and out of barns and fenced or unfenced yards of dirt or grass. As flock sizes became larger, enclosed houses with little to no outside access were introduced (Carter, 1964). By the 1960s, the battery or barren cage system of confinement had become predominant for use with egg laying hens, primarily in the United States, but, eventually, worldwide (Leenstra, et. al., 2016; AVMA, 2012). Litter-bedded floor systems were most commonly used for housing broiler chickens (Shields & Duncan, 2009). Caging egg-laying hens primarily allowed for the use of labor-saving methods to automate feeding, watering, and egg collection, resulting in drastically lowered production costs (Leenstra, et. al., 2016). Evidence also supported their use for the reduction of microbial infections and pecking related injuries (AVMA, 2012). Yet, birds confined in conventional battery cages are allotted an average of 67 square inches of space per bird, an insufficient area to engage in instinctual behaviors such as preening and roosting.

As methods of animal production became more industrial in character, public concern grew with regard to welfare of farm animals. The release of the 1965 Brambell Report, among other research, and the later codification of the "Five Freedoms" for animal welfare, defined basic physical and mental considerations against which animal production systems could be assessed (Conklin, 2014). As a result, in the 1980s the first alternatives to battery cages appeared. These were predominantly free-range barns and what eventually became contemporary *enriched* or *furnished cages,* or the larger *colony cages*. These cages provide more space overall per bird, as well as features that allow birds to meet behavioral needs such as dust baths, scratching, and nesting (Lay, et. al., 2011; Leenstra, et. al., 2016; Shields & Duncan, 2009).

CONFINEMENT SYSTEMS USED IN COMMERCIAL BROILER AND EGG PRODUCTION

The following provides a brief description and general overview of the types of confinement systems used today for commercial production. The benefits and limitations of these systems are discussed.

Standard Battery or Barren Cages

This system of housing is primarily used by the egg industry, and only rarely used as a means to confine meat birds (Sheilds & Duncan, 2009). Standard battery or barren (as referred to in the UK) style cages are wire or metal cages that can house 6-8 birds/cage with limited space per bird of approximately 10 by 10 inches. Battery cages were adopted by egg producers as a labor and cost saving strategy as cages allow for use of automated feed and sanitations and provide sloped flooring to allow for streamlined egg collection. Eggs are generally cleaner than in non-caged systems as chickens are not in contact with manure. Because of this, bacterial and parasitic infections of birds are also reduced. Air quality is better in caged systems that don't involve litter (Nimmermark, Lund, Gustafsson, & Eduard, 2009). Litter leads to airborne particulates, ammonia, and bacteria that increase risk of infections in birds. Smaller group sizes in each cage can reduce the risk of serious pecking injuries, and cages facilitate the monitoring of bird health and wellbeing. However, injurous pecking and cannibalism are a problem with caged as well as uncaged birds, often necessitating the practice of beak trimming (Albentosa & Cooper, 2004).

The primary concern associated with battery cage systems is related to the overall comfort of the birds given that these systems restrict available space for instinctual behaviors such as preening, scratching, nesting, wing flapping, body and tail shaking, and dust bathing (Shields & Greger, 2013). Birds can become trapped in the wire caging and have been shown to more likely experience foot damage and reduced bone density in legs and feet due to inactivity. In the case of meat birds, all caging is associated with an increased risk of chest ulcerations due to their genetic development of large breast muscle. This, coupled with weakened leg bone density, results in birds who lie on their chests all day, resulting in breast blisters and tissue breakdown (Shields & Duncan, 2009; Shields & Greger, 2013).

Enriched, Furnished, or Colony Cage Systems

These confinement systems are used primarily by egg producers and increasingly in broiler production as an alternative to floor systems, though evidence shows that caging meat birds may be more deleterious to their health and welfare (Lay, et. al., 2011; Shields & Duncan, 2009; Shields & Greger, 2013). Many of the concerns related to animal comfort appear to be addressed with the use of these systems. The most significant difference is that these cages offer approximately 20% more space per bird. Or, as one chicken welfare advocate describes it, "a sheet of paper plus a post card" (Barlow, 2019). These confinement systems do provide areas with scratch pads, perches, and nesting boxes, and facilities for dust bathing that allow the birds to engage in instinctual grooming and movement behaviors. In general, they are considered to be a significant improvement over the battery or barren style cages, yet the birds are still standing on metal wire, which increases risk for foot deformities and ulcers. Birds never see the light of day, which some consider inhumane (Barlow, 2019).

Colony cages differ from enriched/furnished cages by the number of birds they can contain (Rodenburg, et. al., 2005). Generally, 10 or fewer birds are kept in enriched/fortified cages, while the bigger colony cages can house up to 60 birds per cage, with the same allotment of space per bird. In other regards, the systems are similar. The additional space and facilities that allow for movement and behaviors have been associated with improved health of the birds, including reduction in injurious pecking and cannibalistic behavior (Huber-Eicher, B., Sebo, 2001; Sherwin, Richards & Nicol, 2010). Perch areas are associated with improved leg strength and foot health (Lay, et. al.,2011), and mortality in this style of housing has been shown to be lower than battery cage, barn/aviary, or free-range systems (Sherwin, et. al., 2010).

Barn or Aviary

This system is generally what is referred to as "cage free" for eggs, and is the predominant means for confining broiler chickens (AVMA, 2012). Barn systems are defined as any enclosed structure where birds are housed on the floor and have access to nesting boxes and litter (Sherwin, et. al., 2010). If the producer can demonstrate access to the outdoors for birds (meaning even one small open door in a larger barn for chickens to go outside), the producer can label their product, usually meat, as "free range" according to USDA guidelines (USDA FSIS, 2019). An aviary is essentially the same as a barn but with the addition of tiered platforms or perches for birds to roost (Huber-Eicher, B., Sebo, 2001). These systems allow greater freedom of movement for birds, but also increase injuries due to landing accidents and illness associated with large flock size (AVMA, 2012).

Benefits associated with barn and aviary system stem from the birds having space for movement. These benefits include improved leg strength and bone density compared with caged animals (Shields & Gregor, 2013), and increased engagement in instinctual behaviors that can reduce stress. However, due to the large flock size, injurious pecking and cannibalism are among the leading causes of injury and mortality to barn or aviary raised birds (Mahboub, Muller, & Von Borell, 2004) For this reason, beak trimming has become a standard practice to prevent pecking. Yet, it is believed that beak trimming is painful for the animal and interferes with its natural functioning (McKenna, 2017). This is an issue for which genetic selection of birds for reduced pecking has shown some promise (Leenstra, et. al., 2017). Compartmentalization of the barn space to reduce flock size has also been shown to ameliorate pecking behaviors (Nicol, et. al., 2006; Shields & Gregor, 2013).

Other risks to birds associated with barn or aviary housing are generally related to infection by fecal borne parasites or infections of eyes and respiratory tracts due to poor air quality (Lay, et. al., 2011; David, Moe, Michel, Lund and Mejdell, 2015). Some studies have shown that mortality can be higher in litter-based systems than in caged systems due to air quality and higher prevalence of parasitic and bacterial infections. Flooring slats, manure collection, and air filtration systems have been shown to ameliorate these problems (David, Moe, Michel, Lund and Mejdell, 2015). Approximately 15% of U.S. commercial egg-layers are "cage free" (UEP, 2017).

Free-Range

As noted above, the key feature of free-range systems is access to the outdoors during the day. These systems can be used with either egg or meat chickens, and they allow for the most extensive array of behavioral opportunities for confined birds (AVMA, 2012). Free-range supports several improved health outcomes such as higher bone density, improved feather condition (Mahboub, Muller, Von Borell, 2004), and reduced signs of stress. But other risks associated with outdoor exposure make chickens more vulnerable, including climatic exposure, predators, toxins, or infections from other wild birds (AVMA, 2012). Details on regulations and requirements for "free range" labeling are discussed below.

Pasture Raised

Pasture raised is generally considered as "non-confined" or "limited confinement" where the animal is allowed continuous access to pasture with natural grasses and wild plants (AWI, 2019). This is the oldest practice of chicken and egg production – simply letting chickens run around the barnyard. Yet, at the same time, due to consumer demand, it is the newest husbandry practice under scrutiny and consideration for development by larger scale chicken producers, primarily to establish guidelines that allow for third party certification and endorsement (Fanatico, Born & Connor, 2002/2010; AWI, 2019).

Pasture raised animals with limited confinement are provided the most opportunity to engage in a full range of instinctual behaviors. Therefore, pasture raised may be considered optimal for animal health and wellbeing. Formal research into the health effects of pastured systems, as well as the effects on the wholesomeness of the meat and egg products, is underway with, as yet, limited and mixed evidence. For example, some studies have shown the nutrient profile of eggs from pasture raised chickens to be superior (PSU, 2010), while, at the same time, the likelihood of microbial contamination may also be increased (AVMA, 2012). In short, more research needs to be done.

CONFINEMENT OF MEAT AND EGG LAYING HENS TODAY

Globally, it is estimated that almost 90% of commercial egg-layers are housed in cages (Leenstra, 2016; HSUS, 2019). *Enriched cages* are used in the European Union (E.U.). The use of standard battery cages was banned in 2012. Approximately 55% of egg layers are housed in enriched cages in the E.U., with the remainder being raised in cage free barns, free ranging outdoors, or pastured (Lay, et. al., 2011; Windhorst, 2016). The U.S. is the largest overall producer of eggs and meat chickens, and among the largest exporters (USDA ERS, 2019). Iowa is the largest poultry producing state. Currently, the use of standard battery cages for egg production in the U.S. has been banned in Rhode Island, California, Massachusettes, Michigan, Ohio, Washington, and Oregon due to animal welfare concerns. Yet, 84% of egg layer hens in the U.S. are still housed in standard battery cages, although interest in adoption of enriched cage systems to address animal welfare concerns and avert cage bans have grown in recent years (Tactacan, Guenter, Lewis, Rodriguez-Lecompte, House, 2009). Approximately 3.2% of egg-laying hens worldwide are kept in free-range or cage-free housing. Interestingly, while the trend in egg production is moving away from caged systems, largely due to consumer demand, the opposite trend is occurring in broiler production, with increased use of cages (Shields & Duncan, 2009; Windhorst, 2016).

Cages used in broiler production are often the enriched, furnished, or colony type (Shields & Greger, 2013). However, some evidence indicates that standard battery cages are commonly in use as well. Cage use for broiler birds is often geographically based and related to access to sources of floor litter or barn size. In both meat and egg production, caging birds allows primarily for reduced costs for feeding, cleaning, and housing more animals per barn, thereby lowering costs on a per bird basis. These cost savings are passed down to consumers, who have come to expect less expensive poultry products.

Much scrutiny has been made of the variable effects of caged versus uncaged confinement systems, particularly for egg production, on both productivity and economic profitability, as well as health and welfare of the animals. Often, these two forces are not in opposition as healthier birds can be more productive layers and less likely to be sick or die (Tactacan, et. al., 2009; Rodenburg, Tuyttens, Sonck, De Reu, Herman, Zoons, 2005; AVMA, 2018). The American Veterinary Medicine Association (2012) and others have described the overall benefits and disadvantages of caged versus free-range systems (Lay, et. al., 2011; Sherwin, Richards & Nicol, 2010). All systems offer some risks and some advantages to both producers and to animals. In general, unconfined systems are more difficult to clean, thereby increasing risk of disease, and larger flocks lead to widespread infections. These systems also require higher labor costs for feeding, watering, and egg collection, and are less conducive to monitoring the wellbeing of individual birds. Confinement systems reduce some of these risks but introduce problems associated with confinement and limited movement. However, of the range of confinement methods, battery cages are generally thought to be most deleterious for animal health and welfare, which has resulted in increased pressure on producers to use alternative systems.

It is important to note that systems of confinement are not the only variable in establishing profitable systems for housing and care of birds that also attend to their welfare needs. Other areas of investigation include breeding and pairing qualities of confinement systems with the varying traits of different breeds of birds (Leenstra, et. al., 2017) and education of the farmers about animal welfare (Appleby & Hughes, 1991; Bestman, 2001). Farmers who better understand the behavioral needs of their chickens and are committed to minimizing risks to their stocks demonstrate reduced illness, stress behaviors, and mortality rates in their flocks (Bestman, 2001).

CAGE FREE, FREE RANGE AND PASTURE RAISED: LABELING REQUIREMENTS AND OVERSIGHT

Public Oversight and Regulation

The USDA is one of the federal regulating bodies for the production and labeling of agricultural products, specifically responsible for meats, poultry, dairy, and eggs. It is important to note that, other than the Human Slaughter of Livestock Regulations Act (9 CFR 313), by comparison with legal protections to domestic pets (dogs, cats, etc.), very little federal legislation governs the welfare of farm animals (HSUS, 2019). Third party agencies generally monitor the care of animals, but this is voluntary on the part of the producer and generally only occurs when the producer is seeking labeling approval or third-party endorsement.

According to the USDA website,

> "In the United States, most livestock production industries have developed and implemented science-based animal care guidelines in response to consumer concerns that animals being raised for food or fiber production are treated humanely. Assurances that animals are being raised according

to these guidelines are provided through voluntary third-party audits rather than legislation." (USDA NAL, n.d.)

With regard to labeling of chicken and eggs pertaining to confinement, the USDA provides definitions for "free range" and" cage free" labeling. In general, "cage free" or "free range" can be used to label either eggs or meat chickens. With regard to eggs, USDA offers guidelines for both labels. However, only "free range" guidelines are stipulated with regard to meat birds. Generally, "cage free" is not a term used for broilers. Neither labels are codified, however, meaning they are only guidelines, not laws. Label definitions from the USDA are as follows:

> "Cage Free: Eggs packed in USDA grade marked consumer packages labeled as cage free must be produced by hens housed in a building, room, or enclosed area that allows for unlimited access to food [and] water, and provides the freedom to roam within the area during the laying cycle." (USDA FSIS, 2015)

USDA guidelines for "free range" eggs are:

> "Free Range: Eggs packed in USDA grade marked consumer packages labeled as free range must be produced by hens housed in a building, room, or area that allows for unlimited access to food [and] water, and continuous access to the outdoors during their laying cycle. The outdoor area may be fenced and/or covered with netting-like material." (USDA FSIS, 2015)

Additionally, the USDA offers minimal stipulation about how, for how long, or what kind of outdoor space birds need to have access to outside of the confinement barn:

> "Producers must demonstrate to the Agency that the poultry has been allowed access to the outside" (USDA FSIS, 2015).

Egg producers whose products are graded by the USDA and wish to include the label "cage-free" or "free range" on the packaging must undergo twice yearly USDA inspection to ensure that hens are housed in the appropriate system for the label (Morris, 2016). There is no federal definition of "pasture-raised" for poultry production in the U.S. at this time.

Private (Third Party) Oversight and Certification

Third party auditors often work in tandem with USDA inspectors (USDA NAL, n.d.; AWI, 2019). Though USDA graded poultry with "cage free" or "free range" undergo twice yearly audits, not all eggs that include "cage free" or "free range" label claims are graded by the USDA. In the case of non-USDA graded products, claims are not verified unless the producer participates in a third-party certification program (AWI, 2019).

There are several private auditing and certification organizations that oversee humane treatment of poultry and other livestock. Some guidelines relate most specifically to requirements of Human Slaughter of Livestock Regulations Act (9 CFR 313), such as those of the National Chicken Council (NCC), which offers Animal Welfare Guidelines and Audit Checklist for Broilers (NCC, 2017). However, the NCC is an industry run organization, so it technically could be considered as not a "third party." The United Egg Producers (UEP) is another industry operated organization (so, hence, may not be "third party") that offers certification and auditing for labeling "cage free," "free range," and "pasture raised." Two third party certifying agencies that are not industry affiliated are Humane Farm Animal Care (HFAC) and the Global Animal Partnership (GAP). These auditors offer certification and endorsement related to several aspects of humane management for poultry including guidelines on beak trimming, handling during the transport and slaughter process, molt programs, and euthanasia of sick animals. A brief discussion of guidelines pertaining to requirements for "cage-free", "free-range," or "pasture raised" for each of these U.S. certifiers is provided below. For more information about other humane handling requirements, information can be found on organization websites.

United Egg Producers

United Egg Producers were the first to develop animal welfare guidelines for the egg industry in the 1980s (UEP, 2017). UEP offers yearly audits, certification, and a product logo for successful industry applicants. Egg producers who apply for "cage-free" status under UEP endorsement are providing barn, aviary, or free-range housing for their birds. Guidelines include a minimum of 1.0 to 1.5 square feet of floor space per bird, water sources to be within 26 feet of all hens, and a minimum of 9 square feet of nest space per 100 birds, as well as guidelines for adequate perch space, litter access, lighting of food and watering areas, and air quality requirements. UEP does not offer certification or audits for "free range" or "pasture raised" labeling.

Humane Farm Animal Care

The nonprofit organization Humane Farm Animal Care (HFAC) offers audits and a "Certified Humane" endorsement for "cage-free", "free-range," and "pasture-raised" meat and egg chickens. In addition to several standards for humane management of chickens (similar to UEP), certification for "free-range" also requires daily access to an uncovered outdoor area that provides a minimum of 2 square feet per bird. Additionally, Certified Humane offers standards for "pasture raised" labeling that requires 2.5 acres per 1,000 birds (HFAC, 2019).

Global Animal Partnership

Global Animal Partnership (GAP) works with other third-party auditors to offer their "Animal Welfare Certified" endorsement for meat and egg laying birds (GAP,

2019). These endorsements cover a variety of types of production methods, as long as minimum standards are met for humane management. GAP endorsements are offered as levels 1-5+based on considerations such as outdoor access, space per bird, lighting, and handling during transport. Level Two offers an "Enriched Environment," which would be the equivalent of "cage free," but with the addition of other animal welfare measures. Levels 3-5+ include the equivalent of "free-range" (level 3) to "pasture-raised" (level 4) and beyond (levels 5 and 5+) (GAP, 2019).

CONCLUSION

As the commercial chicken industry has sought to increase production to match growing demand for eggs and meat, coupled with an increase in consumer awareness of farm animal welfare, systems for more humane housing environments have been devised. Primarily in response to consumer interest, product labeling for chicken meat and eggs now identifies products that are produced in facilities where chickens live in "cage free," "free range," or "pasture raised" environments. Though the evidence to date shows that none of these environments are risk free for the chickens, the general consensus is that they all provide more humane housing for birds than the standard battery or barren cages that are predominantly used by the U.S. egg industry today. The research shows that increased space per chicken, coupled with scratch pads, nesting boxes, perches, and litter, allows birds to engage in natural behaviors, such as grooming, scratching, roosting, and nesting, that are associated with improved animal health. The "cage free" label, therefore, indicates some benefits to the welfare of the chickens. The "free range" label also indicates access to outdoors, which is associated with animal health, although, particularly with USDA certification, the label may be misleading regarding the likelihood that animals actually spend time outside. Finally, "pasture raised" is held by third party auditors to be the highest standard of humane environment for chickens (and other farm animals), as it allows animals to be outside in natural surroundings. However, to date, research is limited regarding the comparative health risks to animals in these production systems.

REFERENCES

Albentosa, M.J., & Cooper, J.J. "Effects of cage height and stocking density on the frequency of comfort behaviors performed by laying hens housed in furnished cages." *Anim Wel* 13 (2004): 419-424.

American Veterinary Medicine Association [AVMA] (2012) *Literature Review on Welfare Implications of Laying Hen Housing.* Retrieved from https://www.avma.org/KB/Resources/Literature Reviews/Documents/laying_hen_housing_bgnd.pdf.

Animal Welfare Institute [AWI] (2019), *A Consumer's Guide to Food Labels and Animal Welfare.* Retrieved from https://awionline.org/content/consumers-guide-food-labels-and-animal-welfare

Appleby, M.C., Hughes B.O. "Welfare of laying hens in cages and alternative systems: environmental, physical and behavioral aspects." *World's Poultry Science Journal*, 47, no.2 (1991):109-28.

Barlow J. (2019) *Enriched and Colony Cages.* Retrieved from https://poultrykeeper.com/rehoming-battery-hens/enriched-and-colony-cages/

Bestman M.W.P (2001)."The Role of Management and Housing in the Prevention of Feather Pecking in Laying Hens." In: Hovi M and Bouilhol M (eds.), *Human-Animal Relationship: Stockmanship and Housing in Organic Livestock Systems. Proceedings of the Third NAHWOA Workshop, Clermont-Ferrand, France: Network for Animal Health and Welfare in Organic Agriculture* (pp.77-86), Reading, United Kingdon: University of Reading.

Bray, H.J., Ankeny R.A. (2017). "Happy Chickens Lay Tastier Eggs: Motivations for Buying Free-range Eggs in Australia." *Anthrozoös* 30 (2): 213-226.

Carter, C.T. "Modern Trends in Animal Health and Husbandry: Poultry Breeding". *British Veterinary Journal* 120 (1964): 506-517.

Clauer P. (2012). Pennsylvania State University. *The Modern Egg Industry.* Retrieved from https://extension.psu.edu/modern-egg-industry.

Conklin, T. (2014) *An Animal Welfare History Lesson on the Five Freedoms.* Michigan State University Extension. Retrieved from https://www.canr.msu.edu/news/an_animal_welfare_history_lesson_on_the_five_freedoms.

David, B. Moe, R.O., Michel, V., Lund, V. and Mejdell, C. (2005) Air Quality in Alternative Housing Systems May Have an Impact on Laying Hen Welfare. Part I—Dust. *Animal.* 5 no.3 (2005): 495–511.

Fanatico, A., Born, H. & Connor, B. (2002/2010) *Label Rouge: Pasture- Based Poultry Production in France.* National Sustainable Agriculture Information Service. Retrieved from http://citeseerx.ist.psu.edu/viewdoc/download?doi=10.1.1.682.3928&rep=rep1&type=pdf

Global Animal Partnership [GAP] (2019) *Producers.* Retrieved from https://globalanimal partnership.org/producers/.

Huber-Eicher, B., Sebo, (2001) F. "Reducing feather pecking when raising laying hen chicks in aviary systems." *Applied Animal Behavior Science*, no.1-2 (2001): 59-68.

Humane Farm Animal Care [HFAC] (2019) *Our Standards.* Retrieved from https://certifiedhumane.org/how-we-work/our-standards/

Humane Society of the United States [HSUS] (2019) *Improving the Lives of Farm Animals.* Retrieved from https://www.humanesociety.org/all-our-fights/protect-farm-animals

———. (2019). *Cage Free versus Battery Cage Eggs.* Retrieved from https://www.humanesociety.org/resources/cage-free-vs-battery-cage-eggs.

Lay, D. C., Fulton, R.M., Hester, P.Y., Karcher, D.M., Kjaer, K.B., Mench, J.A., Mullens, I., Newberry, R.C., Nicol, C.J., O'Sullivan, N.P., and Porter, R.E., "Hen Welfare in Different Housing Systems." *Poultry Science* 90 (2011): 278–294.

Leenstra, F., Ten Napel, J., Visscher, J. & Van Sambeek, F. "Layer Breeding Programmes in Changing Production Environments: a historic perspective." *World's Poultry Science Journal*, 72, no. 1 (2016): 21-36.

Lyson, T.A. (2012) Civic Agriculture: Reconnecting Farm, Food and Community. Boston, MA: Tufts University Press.

Mahboub, H.D.H., Muller, J., Von Borell, E., "Outdoor Use, Tonic Immobility, Heterophil/Lymphocyte Ratio and Feather Condition in Free-Range Laying Hens of Different Genotype." *British Poultry Science,* 45 (2004): 738-744.

McKenna, M. (2017) Big Chicken: The Incredible Story of How Antibiotics Created Modern Agriculture and Changed the Way the World Eats. Washington, D.C: National Geographic Books.

Messer, K.D., Costanigro, M., Kaiser, H.M. (2017). "Labeling Food Processes: The Good, the Bad and the Ugly." *Applied Economic Perspectives and Policy* 39 no.3 (2017): 407–427.

Morris, C. (2016) *USDA Graded Cage Free Eggs: All They're Cracked Up to Be.* Retrieved from https://www.usda.gov/media/blog/2016/09/13/usda-graded-cage-free-eggs-all-theyre-cracked-be

National Chicken Council [NCC] (2017) *National Chicken Council Animal Welfare Guidelines And Audit Checklist For Broilers.* Retrieved from https://www.nationalchickencouncil.org/wp-content/uploads/2017/07/NCC-Welfare-Guidelines-Broilers.pdf

Nicol, C.J., Brown, S.N., Glen, E., Pope, S.J.,Short, F.J, Warriss, P.D., Zimmerman, P.H., & Wilkins, L.J., "Effects of stocking density, flock size and management on the welfare of laying hens in single-tier aviaries." *British Poultry Science,* 47, no.2 (2006): 135-46.

Nimmermark, S., Lund, V., Gustafsson, G. & Eduard, W., "Ammonia, Dust and Bacteria in Welfare-oriented Systems for Laying Hens."Annals of Agricultural and Environmental Medicine. 16, (2009): 103-113.

Pennsylvania State University News [PSU] (2010), *Research Shows Eggs From Pastured Chickens May be More Nutritious.* Retrieved from https://news.psu.edu/story/166143/2010/07/20/research-shows-eggs-pastured-chickens-may-be-more-nutritious

Rodenburg, T.B., Tuyttens, F.A., Sonck, B., De Reu, K., Herman, L., Zoons, J., "Welfare, Health, and Hygiene of Laying Hens Housed in Furnished Cages and in Alternative Housing Systems." *Journal of Applied Animal Welfare Science.* 8, no.3 (2005): 211-226.

Sherwin CM, Richards GJ, Nicol CJ.(2010). "A Comparison of the Welfare of Layer Hens in Four Housing Systems in the UK." *British Poultry Science.* 51, no.4 (2010): 488-499.

Shields, S. & Duncan, I.J.H (2009). "A Comparison of the Welfare of Hens in Battery Cages and Alternative Housing Systems." *The Humane Society Institute for Science and Policy Animal Studies Repository. Retrieved from* https://animalstudiesrepository.org/cgi/viewcontent.cgi?article=1014&context=hsus_reps_impacts_on_animals .

Shields, S. & Greger, M., "Animal Welfare and Food Safety Aspects of Confining Broiler Chickens to Cages." *Animals,* 3, no.2 (2013): 386-400.

Tactacan, G.B., Guenter, W., Lewis, N.J., Rodriguez-Lecompte, J.C., House, J.D. "Performance and Welfare of Laying Hens in Conventional and Enriched Cages." *Poultry Science.* 88, no.4 (2009): 698-707.

United Egg Producers [UEP] (2017) *Animal Husbandry Guidelines for U.S. Egg- Laying Flocks.* Retrieved from https://uepcertified.com/wp-content/uploads/2015/08/2016-UEP-Animal-Welfare-Guidelines-2016-Cage-Free-Edit-002.pdf

United States Department of Agriculture, Economic Research Service [USDA ERS], *Poultry and Eggs.* Retrieved from https://www.ers.usda.gov/topics/animal-products/poultry-eggs/.

United States Department of Agriculture, Food Safety Inspection Service [USDA FSIS] (2015) *Meat and Poultry Labeling Terms.* Retrieved from https://www.fsis.usda.gov/wps/portal/fsis/topics/food-safety-education/get-answers/food-safety-fact-sheets/food-labeling/meat-and-poultry-labeling-terms/meat-and-poultry-labeling-terms

United States Department of Agriculture, National Agricultural Lbirary [USDA NAL] n.d. Retrieved from https://www.nal.usda.gov/awic/animal-welfare-audit-and-certification-programs.

U.S. Poultry and Egg Association [USPEA] (2019). Retrieved from http://www.uspoultry.org/about/history.cfm.

Windhorst H.W (2016) *Housing Systems and Egg Production – 2016 Status Report.* Retrieved from https://zootecnicainternational.com/focus-on/housing-systems-egg-production-2016-status-report/.

CHAPTER 6

Labels: Keys to the Success of Consumer Buycotts

Jamille Palacios Rivera (University of Missouri)

ABSTRACT

Farm workers in the U.S. have used boycotts and strikes as tactics to improve their wages and working conditions. Strikes are not as common for these workers as boycotts because the National Labor Relations Act excludes the agricultural sector. Only a few states have regulated unionization and consumer boycotts as collective bargaining tactics in the sector. Although the list of boycott efforts led by farm workers is rather large, the tactic's success is mixed. Currently, the Coalition of Immokalee Workers (CIW) is leading a boycott effort called the "Fair Food" campaign. The campaign voices that commodity buyers perpetuate unfair, illegal, and unhuman farm labor practices, and calls for consumer support via boycotts. While the boycott is effective in negatively affecting the boycott target, it also affects the farm workers leading the boycott because farmworkers are inputs in the production of the boycotted product and input demands are derived from final product demands. In contrast, targets ending the boycott agree to participate in the Fair Food Program (FFP). Participation in this unique program requires a premium rate over the price of the agricultural commodity, and preference to commodity growers establishing and following the FFP's supplier code of conduct. The premium rate is typically a penny per pound of the commodity purchased. It supports farmworkers' wages and sponsors human rights educational and advocacy programs. The FFP's components make it unique. None of the previous boycott termination agreements imposed a code of conduct as condition to supply farm products, nor included a premium paid by retailers to supplement farmworkers' wages and support training programs. Under the program, the Fair Food Standard Council audits growers; those following the "Supplier Code of Conduct" or buying commodities from certified growers are certified as Fair Food and receive a label. Although participating in the FFP is costly, the label offers a marketing opportunity. Buycotts occur from consumers' support to companies perceived as acting responsibly. The magnitude of the impact on farm workers depends on consumers' boycott and buycott. This chapter shows the Fair Food label claim and importance of consumer support in the success of the boycott and buycotts.

FARM WORKERS' WAGES AND WORKING CONDITIONS

Agriculture is among the top five industries in the U.S. Department of Labor (DOL) - Wage and Hour Division (WHD) list of industries with low wages and high labor law violations. [1] The average farm wage rate estimated using the most recently available data published by National Agricultural Workers Survey (NAWS) is $11.21/hour. That wage rate is above the federal minimum wage, but below the average hourly wage rate for the U.S. agricultural industry at $12.98 reported by the Bureau of Labor Statistics (BLS) (shown in Figure 1). This wage rate is 43.6 percent the per hour wage rate received by production workers in private non-agricultural industries (Figure 2). This percentage fits within the range persistently displayed even after the 1978 amendments to the Fair Labor Standards Act eliminating the difference between the federal minimum wage rate for agriculture and nearly the rest of the labor markets (Figure 3).

Figure 1 - Average Annual Minimum Wage Rate versus Average Market Wages
(Agricultural, Non-agricultural, and NAWS)

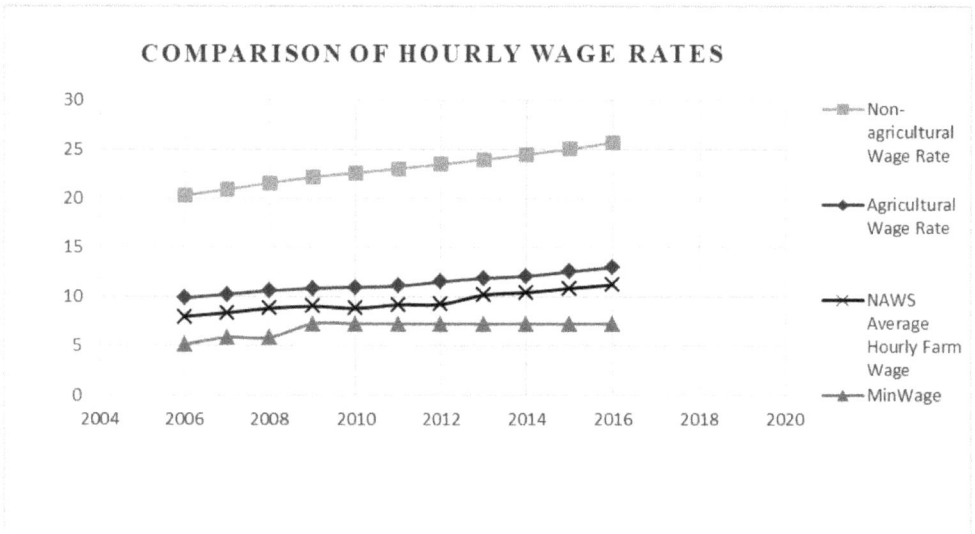

---

[1] "Fiscal Year Data for WHD," U.S. Department of Labor, https://www.dol.gov/whd/data/datatables.htm [accessed 11 March 2020].

Figure 2 – Agriculture to Non-agriculture Market Wage Rate Ratio (1950 to 2008)

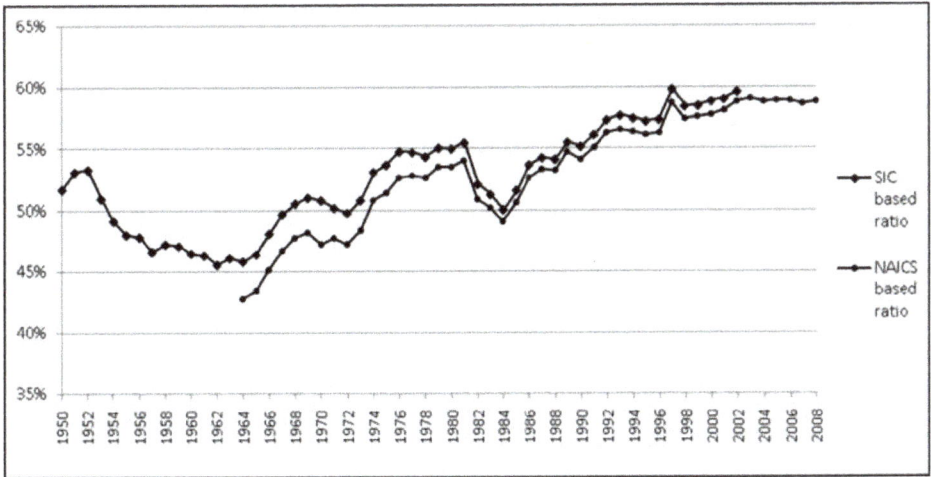

Figure 3 – Agriculture to Non-agriculture Market Wage Rate Ratio (2008 - 2016)[2]

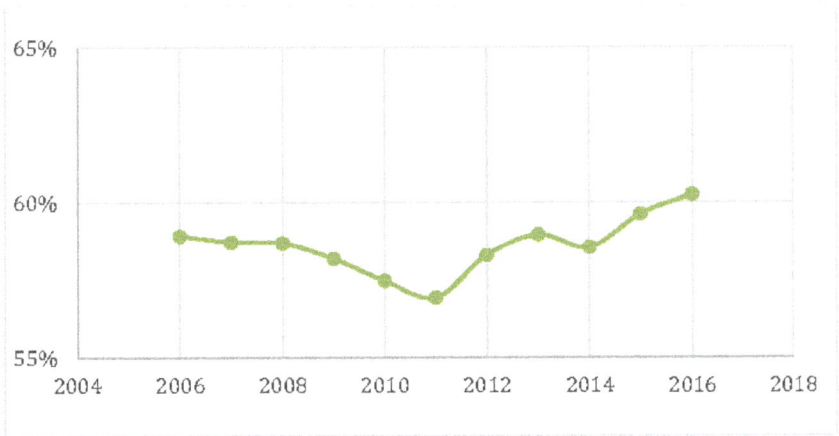

---

[2] Note: The ratio for the years 1950 to 2003 was obtained using the farm labor average wage rate from the Farm Labor Reports (USDA-NASS), and the hours and earnings in private nonagricultural industries reported in the 1991 and 2003 Economic Report of the President (EOP) (Tables B-44 and B-47, respectively) (EOP 1991 and 2003); data are based on the Standard Industrial Classification (SIC). The 1964 to 2008 ratio uses the farm labor average wage rate from the Labor Reports (USDA-NASS), and the hours and earnings in private nonagricultural industries reported in the 2009 Economic Report of the President (Table B-47) (EOP 2009); data are based on the North American Industry Classification System (NAICS).

The wage rates in the statistics above are for domestic workers. The farm labor market is segmented. Some workers in U.S. fields are non-resident foreigners with H2-A visas. They are brought from a foreign country to perform a temporary or seasonal agricultural labor or service. They receive a federally established wage rate called Adverse Effect Wage Rate (AEWR) to minimize the effects from increasing labor supply in this market. Employers demonstrate labor shortages from difficulties in finding domestic workers to perform fieldwork before their job positions are certified for H2-A workers. Those hiring them follow certain requirements. At the present, employers provide H2-A workers with housing, medical care, and transportation from worker housing to the job site. Users have criticized this type of guest workers program as burdensome and costly, which explains its under- or mis-utilization.

But even with the regulations and the wage and hour division enforcement activities, a study by the Urban Institute and Northeastern University reports that over 71% of labor trafficking and slavery victims in the United States came with H2-A**Invalid source specified.**. Slavery victims are physically abused and forced to work past their authorized time. More often than ideally, growers are ordered to pay back wages and monetary penalties for violating the Fair Labor Standard Act (FLSA) or failing to meet H-2A requirements. WHD, DOL enforcement data show that at least since 2000, farmers have paid between $900,000.00 and almost $8 million in annual back wages and civil monetary penalties (Figure 4). A significant percent of the 2016 total paid back wages and civil monetary penalties were for H-2A violations; 47% and 52%, respectively (WHD, DOL, 2017).

Figure 4 – Back wages and civil monetary penalties in agriculture

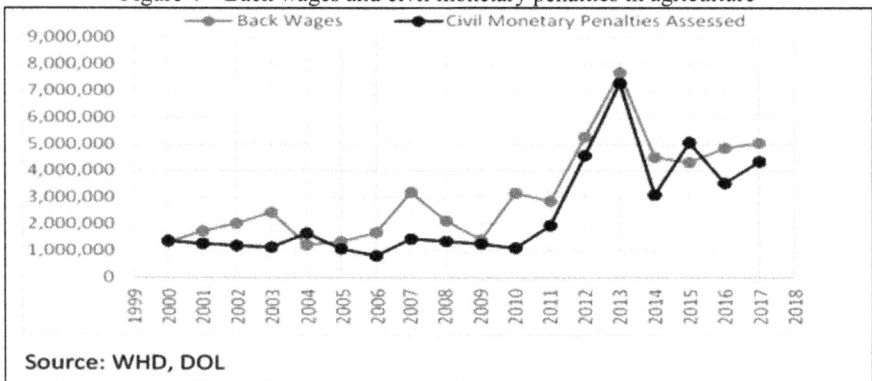

Source: WHD, DOL

BOYCOTTS AND STRIKES

Workers have demanded better wage rates and working conditions, but growers' willingness and ability to pay higher wage rates and improve working conditions depends upon commodity prices set under competitive forces. To pressure growers, workers rely on boycotts and strikes. Boycotts are more common than strikes for these workers because the National Labor Relations Act, a federal law that establishes labor rights and regulates unionization, excludes agriculture and related sectors. A few states have enacted legal provisions or prohibitions regarding the right to unionize or the use of consumer boycotts as a collective bargaining tactic in the sector. Although the list of boycott efforts led by farm workers is extensive, the tactic's success is mixed.

Table 1 lists some boycott efforts from 1966 to 2007, not in chronological order, but by farmworker's group (Palacios 2017). Three main farm labor groups have led boycott efforts and strikes. United Farm Workers (UFW) led 13 of these boycott efforts. The majority of them, 11, against California grapes and lettuce producers and impacting strong brand names such as Sun Harvest, Lucky Stores, and Gallo Wine; the other two boycotts were against Florida citrus producers and the Coca-Cola brand name. The Farm Labor Organizing Committee (FLOC) follows, with boycott efforts in Michigan, Ohio, and North Carolina. FLOC's targets were cucumber, tomato, and tobacco producers, and respective associated marketing brand names: Campbell's, Mount Olive Pickle Company, and RJ Reynolds. One other group of workers, the Pineros y Campesinos Unidos (PCUN) led a boycott effort in Oregon against NORPAC Foods and fruit and vegetable growers.

Table 1 – List of boycotts and strikes by farm worker's groups (1966 to 2007)

Group	Firm	Strategy	Product	State	Year
UFW United Farm Workers					
	DiGiorgio Fruit	Strike/boycott	Fruit/vegetables	CA	1966 1966
	Schenley Vineyards	Strike/boycott	Grapes	CA	1966 - 1966
	Perelli-Minetti Winery, Christian Bro, & Almaden	Strike/boycott	Grapes	CA	1966 - 1970
	Guimarra Vineyards	Strike/boycott	Grapes	CA	1967 - 1970
	Bud Antle Lettuce	Boycott	Lettuce	CA	1970 - n/a
	Coca-Cola	Strike/boycott	Citrus	FL	1972 - 1972
	Coca-Cola	Strike/boycott	Citrus	FL	1975 - n/a
	Grapes, lettuce & Gallo Wine	Boycott	Grapes/lettuce	CA	1973 - 1978
	Lucky Stores	Boycott	Lettuce	CA	1980 - n/a
	Sun Harvest	Strike/boycott	Lettuce	CA	1979 - 1979
	Bruce Church, Inc	Boycott	Lettuce	CA	1979 - n/a
	Grapes	Boycott	Grapes	CA	1983 - 1992
	E &J Gallo Winery	Boycott	Grapes	CA	2005 - 2005
FLOC Farm Labor Organizing Committee					-
	Campbell's Soup/Libby	Strike	Tomato/cucumber	OH/MI	1978 - 1985
	Campbell's Vlasic	Boycott	Cucumber	MI	1983 - 1986
	Mount Olive Pickle Co.	Boycott	Cucumber	NC	1997 - 2004
	RJ Reynolds	Boycott	Tobacco	NC	2007 - n/a
PCUN Pineros y Campesinos Unidos					
	Kraemer Farms	Strike	Cucumber	OR	1991 - n/a
	NORPAC Foods, Inc	Boycott	Fruit/vegetables	OR	1992 - 2002
	Strawberry industry	Strike	Strawberry	OR	1995 - 1995
	Nature's Fountain	Strike		OR	n/a - 1998

Source: Palacios 2017

THE FAIR FOOD CAMPAIGN

Farm workers' hope is on a recent tactic, the Fair Food campaign, a consumer boycott led by the Coalition of Immokalee Workers (CIW). This is a worker-based human rights organization founded in Immokalee, Florida. This geographic area produces a significant percent of the nation's winter harvested tomatoes for the fresh market, and also bell peppers, cucumbers, and citrus. The CIW campaign voices that commodity buyers perpetuate unfair, sometimes illegal, and unhuman farm labor practices, and calls for consumer support via boycotts. The list of commodity buyers targeted by the Fair Food campaign is in Table 2 (Palacios 2017).

Only some of the commodity buyers targeted by the Fair Food campaign are food retailers selling directly to final consumers; those are directly exposed to consumer boycotts. The rest are their input suppliers at intermediary sectors of the food marketing chain or system. This other group, including commodity processors, distributors, and packagers is not the focus of the analysis.

Table 2 – List of Boycott Efforts by CIW under Fair Food Campaign

CIW	Target	Start	Buycott
	Taco Bell (only)	2001	2005
	Rest of Yum! Brands	2005	2007
	McDonald's & Chipotle	2005	2007
	SIC 5812 Fast-food	2005	n/a
	Burger King	2005	2008
	Wendy's	2005	n/a
	Subway	2005	2008
	Chipotle (after IPO)	2006	2012
	Whole Foods	2008	2008
	Walmart	2008	2015
	Winn Dixie	2008	n/a
	Kroger	2008	n/a
	Safeway	2008	n/a
	Supervalu	2008	n/a
	Publix	2008	n/a
	Sysco	2008	n/a
	US Food Service	2008	n/a
	Aramark	2009	2010

CIW	Target	Start	Buycott
	Chartwells	2009	2009
	Sodexo	2009	2010
	Ahold (USA)	2009	2015
	Fresh Market		2015
	Trader Joe's		2012
	Compas Group		2009
	Bonapetit Management Company		2009

Data source: Palacios 2017

Taco Bell was the first Fair Food Campaign target and the first to end boycott efforts by participating in the "Fair Food" program (FFP). Although they entered the program in 2005, labels were not yet part of the program.

Taco Bell was a subsidiary of Yum! Brands, Inc. Of all Yum! Brands subsidiaries, only Taco Bell had been targeted. Once Taco Bell joined in 2005, the remaining subsidiaries at the time—Pizza Hut, KFC, and Long John Silvers—were also targeted. These joined the program soon after. In 2005, the CIW targeted McDonalds and Chipotle Mexican Grill. At the time Chipotle was a subsidiary of McDonalds. Chipotle is now a stand-alone publically traded corporation. McDonalds entered the program in 2007, and Chipotle in 2012. The campaign gained traction after the group announced boycott efforts against the entire food industry. In 2008, they launched direct boycott efforts against other fast food chains, grocery stores, and distributors. Some ended the boycotts, others continue under boycott efforts. The list of food companies who have not yet ended boycott efforts by participating in the FFP includes Wendy's, U.S. Food Service, Sysco, and groceries stores operating in highly concentrated markets.

The Fair Food program expanded from Florida to other states and from tomatoes to other crops, perhaps because of the large scope of the efforts and nature of the industry. Many farmworkers migrate, and farm owners operate in multiple states and are diversified. As of 2019 the program covers farms in Maryland, New Jersey, the Carolinas, Georgia, and Florida. The specialty crops covered by the "Fair Food" program have been expanded from tomatoes to include strawberries and peppers. Growers participating in the Fair Food program include Del Monte, DiMare, Santa Sweets, Sunripe, Limpman, and Lady Moon. Although program participation is at its highest level, campaigns continue against Wendy's, Publix, and others.

Table 3 – Fair Food Participating Retailers and Growers

Participant Growers	Participants in the Marketing Sector
Del Monte Fresh Production	Ahold USA (Alhold Delhaize)
DiMare Ruskin/DiMare Fresh/DiMare Homestead	Aramark
Lady Moon Farms	Bon Appetit Management Co.
Lipman Produce (Tomatoes and Green Bell Peppers	Burger King
in FL, SC, VA, MD	Chipotle Mexican Grill
Pacific Tomato/Strawberries Growers d/b/a Sunripe	Compass Group
Certified Brands (GA, FL)	The Fresh Market
Artesian Farms	McDonald's
Big Red Tomato Packers	Sodexo
Ag-Mart Produce d/b/a Santa Sweets (FL, NC, and NJ	Subway
	Trader Joe's
	Wal-Mart
	Whole Foods Market
	Yum! Brands

Source: Palacios 2017

Imagine the coordination challenge that the Fair Food Program faced as more boycott targets entered the program. Perhaps, that explains the creation of the Fair Food Standards Council (FFSC) in 2011. The FFSC coordinates the flow of the monetary supplement through the food marketing chain, from the retailer participant to farm workers. It also monitors supplier code of conduct compliance, manages implementation of human rights education programs, and offers a hotline for farmworkers to report human rights violations. The Council also certifies grower participation and provides labels.

Participation in this unique program requires a premium rate over the price of the agricultural commodity, and preference to commodity growers establishing and following the FFP's supplier code of conduct. The premium rate is typically a penny per pound of the commodity purchased. It supports farmworker wages and sponsors human rights educational and advocacy programs. The Fair Food Standards Council's website indicates that about $20 million has been collected from and invested in the program, but the amount to supplement wage rates is unknown.

The supplier code of conduct requires, but is not limited to, the following: a grower payroll system to track working hours accurately, labor and safety related training for supervisors and farmworkers, the provision of appropriate bathrooms, pesticide application education, and shade structures for farm workers in the field. None of the previous boycott termination agreements in Table 1 imposed a code of conduct as a condition to supply farm products, nor included a premium paid by retailers to supplement farmworker wages and support training programs. Under the program, the Fair Food Standard Council audits growers; those following the "Supplier Code of Conduct" or buying commodities from certified growers are certified as Fair Food and receive a label. Although participating in the FFP is costly, the label brings to program participants an opportunity for a "buycott."

Buycotts occur from consumer support to sellers perceived as acting responsibly. Sandovici and Davis (2010) define buycotting as "the deliberate act of purchasing a product to support specific ethical, moral or political concerns" with the potential to "generate societal and political change." Although their article points at recent proliferation of companies going organic, contributing to safer environments, and pledging revenue portions toward supporting a societal cause as demonstration of activism's market impact, this is not new. Friedman's (1996) study identifies buycott initiatives conducted since the 1930s. These initiatives were fragmented, less frequent than boycotts, and were not called buycotts. Other names use for buycotts, in Friedman's paper and others, include: "political consumerism", "procott", "reverse boycott", and "anti-boycott." Friedman says that the consumer buycott term "should not be used to refer to pro-buying initiatives with a profit-making orientation." His paper establishes a framework for the success of buycotts starting by making a fundamental distinction between actual buycotts and direct or indirect calls for buycotts. According to Friedman's definition, both should be made by nonprofit organizations. Actual buycotts are campaigns launched, at boycott intensity level, to persuade consumers to buy approved products. Calls for buycotts have the same objective, but use lighter tactics identifying companies supporting a cause or behaving responsibly.

Labels, or "seals of approval," assist in calls for buycotts and actual buycott campaigns. They typically identify recommended products for supporting a specific cause. "Published lists or seals of approval are often a necessary, but insufficient, step to alter well-established consumer purchase behaviors; and advertising or promotional campaign is usually needed to make the message actionable" Friedman (1996). A recent effective campaign involving labels include the Fair Trade campaign. A Belgian study, for instance, found that surveyed consumers are willing to pay a 10 percent premium price for fair-trade coffee (De Pelsmacker, Driesen, & Rayp, 2005). This is consistent with the results of a study by Loureiro and Lotade from 2005. They showed that consumers are willing to pay a higher price for coffee labeled as fair trade and grown under shade. Consumers are leaning toward sustainable foods, which include those produced ensuring "a safe and hygienic working environment and high social welfare and training for all employees involved in the food chain" (Smith, 2008). Such activities have a positive influence on a company's reputation and on its internal and external relationships (Heyder and Theuvsen 2012; Vidales, Vargas and Garcia 2012; Mazur-Wierzbicka 2015; F. M. Roka 2016; Roka and Guan 2018).

The Fair Food label (https://www.fairfoodprogram.org/), for instance, is green, identifies farm workers' fair practices as the cause, and communicates workers' approval of final food products. It serves the CIW buycott call and Fair Food campaign. Positively impacting the demand for Fair Food commodities, which are fresh farm products, is essential for the cause because the beneficiaries of this campaign are farm workers involved in the production and harvesting of these commodities. A challenge for this case is that these commodities are purchased directly and indirectly by consumers; they are sold directly to consumers at farmer markets and indirectly via fresh produce retailers, processed food retailers, and as part of a meal at restaurants. The label will only be apparent to consumers when buying the fresh farm commodity either directly from farmers or indirectly from FFP approved retailers (i.e. FFP participant groceries stores). It is not apparent to consumers when buying processed food from retailers or restaurants. As noted, the Fair Food buycott has multiple targets and is considered direct when targeting farmers selling directly to final consumers and indirect when targeting fresh produce retailers, food restaurants, and processed food manufacturers, distributors, and retailers. Friedman refers to indirect buycotts as surrogate and direct buycotts as nonsurrogate.

MULTI-LEVEL MARKET MODEL FOR SURROGATE BOYCOTTS AND BUYCOTTS

Any decrease in the demand for processed food products due to a boycott, indirectly impacts the demand for commodities used as inputs, and consequently affects farm labor markets. This is because farm worker's demand is derived from the demand for farm products. An effective buycott does the opposite. It increases the targeted product's demand at the final consumer market, consequently increasing the demand for the commodity. Any positive impacts inflicted by buycotts on the demand for commodities bring positive results for farm workers employed under the Fair Food program. These summarize the results of a Gardner's multi-level market model application by Palacios (2013). The model set-up and results are developed in this section. The results show how buycotts supporting fairer labor practices could be an effective tactic in improving working conditions and wage rates for farm workers. The magnitude of the impact depends on output and input elasticities, as well as cost shares.

Gardner's multi-level market model, as in Palacios (2013), begins by establishing a profit maximization problem for two industries, retail (r) and grower (g). Both industries are characterized as competitive, profit maximizing, and having two types of inputs and one output.[3]

$$\text{Max.} \quad \pi^r = P_y Y - P_X X - P_c c + \lambda^r [Y - \varphi^r(X, c)] \quad \text{(1-0a)}$$

$$\text{Max.} \quad \pi^g = P_X X - P_L L - P_z z + \lambda^g [X - \varphi^g(L, z)] \quad \text{(1-0b)}$$

Three additional assumptions are necessary: (1) all commodities are inputs going to retailers that are either boycott or buycott targets; and (2) workers are labor input at grower market.

The "retailer" is a member of the food marketing system considered an intermediary offering a fresh or processed food product to final consumers. The fresh or processed food product sold by retailers is represented by (Y) in Equation 1-0a. At that market level, there are two inputs. The first is input (X), a farm product (commodity). The second input, c, is an aggregate of all other necessary inputs for the final food product. Prices for inputs c and X and for the output Y are P_c, P_x, and P_Y, respectively. In the grower-level profit maximization equation, (1-0b), the output is the farm commodity (X) demanded as input by the retailer selling food

---

[3] The assumption on the number of inputs and outputs is for convenience to simplify the model development. This can be relaxed to consider other interesting situations.

products to final consumers. Two types of inputs are assumed at the farm level. Farm labor is the first, for which units are represented by (L). The second is an aggregate of all remaining necessary farm inputs, represented by (z). P_L, P_z, and P_x are the prices for inputs and output, respectively. The λ^i are the Lagrange multipliers associated with well-behaved production functions at both levels, $\varphi^r(X,c)$ and $\varphi^g(L,z)$.[4]

Equations 1-1a through 1-5a and 1-1b through 1-5b represent the structural model of food retailer and commodity growers under profit maximization, respectively.

$$Y = \varphi^r(X,c) \qquad (1.1a)$$

$$P_X = \varphi^r_X P_Y \qquad (1-2a)$$

$$P_c = \varphi^r_c P_Y \qquad (1-3a)$$

$$c = g(P_c) \qquad (1-4a)$$

$$Y = D(P_Y) \qquad (1-5a)$$

$$X = \varphi^g(L,z) \qquad (1-1b)$$

$$P_L = \varphi^g_L P_X \qquad (1-2b)$$

$$P_z = \varphi^g_z P_X \qquad (1-3b)$$

$$L = \pounds(P_L) \qquad (1-4b)$$

$$z = h(P_z) \qquad (1-5b)$$

Boycott support from consumers shows a move away from the final food product. In other words, the presence of an effective boycott decreases the final product demand in Equation 1-5a. The new demand equation is $Y = D(P_Y) - B$. In this equation, B represents boycotted quantities of the final product. For the buycott analysis, it is assumed that consumers are made aware of producer's participation on the FFP by a label on fresh products and other effective Fair Food boycott campaign efforts targeting processed food retailers and restaurants. With enough consumer awareness and support comes an effective buycott. The demand for the food product is restated to the pre-boycott level. This assumption is plausible given the results of Sandovici and Davis (2010) study indicating that "individuals who are likely to participate in boycotts do not differ in any systematic way from those most likely to participate in buycotts. Individuals who deliberately purchase a product for political, ethical, or environmental reasons and individuals who choose not to

---

[4] This is from the final assumption that the technology for both industries is linear homogeneous.

purchase a product for the same reasons appear very much alike in terms of individual attributes." But a premium per product purchased in support of the farm workers' cause may improve farm working conditions. To show the buycott effects on all sectors, including farmworkers, two equations are modified:

Equation 1-2a becomes
$$P_X = \frac{P_Y \varphi_X^r}{V}$$

Equation 1-4b becomes $L=\pounds(w)$.

The letter V in the modified Equation 1-2a represents percent change in the monetary support (premium) over the market price of the "Fair" farm product. The labor equation now distinguishes the labor demand wage rate from the labor supply wage rate which is supplemented by the Fair Food premium.

RESULTS

Long-run effects of changes in boycott and buycott support are examined as percentage changes by mathematically solving the system of equations corresponding to the profit maximization problems previously established. The set of percent change equations and assumed parameter values are in the appendix.

Table 4 – Multi-level Market Model Results

	Boycott	Buycott
EY/ E	-0.49	0.017
EP$_\sqrt{}$/E	-0.10	-0.003
EX/E	-0.43	0.121
EP$_X$/E	-0.16	-1.108
EL/E	-0.49	1.703
EP$_L$/E	-0.10	-2.69

Table 4 includes some of the results of the analysis, assuming a relatively elastic supply for farm labor (e_L=5) and a less elastic supply for z (e_z = 2). A percent change in boycott support reduces the demand for the food product; that is, the long-run equilibrium is at a lower price point. This impacts growers' markets as follows: lower equilibrium quantities demanded and lower prices. The consequent result for farm workers is also negative with lower units of labor demanded and lower wage rates.

Under an effective buycott or call for buycott, consumers are made aware of fair practices by food retailers (fresh food retailers, processed and fresh food grocery stores, and restaurants) restoring demand to pre-boycott levels. For that, retailers are willing to pay a premium amount over the fresh farm product to support the farm labor cause, as if that input was taxed. The preference toward the "fairer" farm product pressures the market price for the final food product slightly down. Based on the parameters assumed, the market price for food products sold by retailers decreases by .003 percent. This effect transfers to the growers' market level to a higher extend to offset the premium amount over the price for fair farm products. Retailers increase the demand for commodities grown under the supplier code of conduct, but to pay about 1.11 percent less per commodity unit. Growers, then, demand more farmworkers (1.7 percent), but because of the supplemental wage rate under the FFP there is an increase in labor supply pushing the farm labor market wage rate down, 2.69 percent lower. However, the premium amount paid over the final food product supplements farm workers' income.

CONCLUSIONS

Boycotts and buycotts affect sellers of final products, but also input suppliers. Input suppliers' impact from boycotts may be higher than that inflicted on the sellers at the final consumer markets. When the input suppliers are the interest group, such as in this case, there is a counterintuitive result. Supporting the boycott hurts the very people for whom the efforts are led.

A buycott paired with a premium amount over the farm product market price seems effective in helping farm worker's cause. An effective label influences buyers toward purchasing "fair" fresh commodities and paying a premium amount over the market price. Unfortunately, labels are not options for the indirect component of the Fair Food buycott. For that, the CIW enters into agreements with buyers to purchase from approved farm product suppliers. The Fair Food label for this case is used as the buycott campaign logo and participation in the program should be promoted by commodity buyers (food processor) participating in the FFP. These are considered effective as long as they influence consumer's willingness to not only purchase the product, but pay a premium to support the FFP and supplement farm workers' wage rates.

The results at all market levels depend on final product elasticity, input elasticities, cost shares, and other additional factors. Here, the labor supply is assumed to be highly elastic. Although the elasticity value assumed is consistent with elasticities found empirically for farm labor markets, this can change. Consider, for instance, the demographics of the current U.S. farm labor, and tighter immigration policies reducing the supply of labor in this market. This not only may decrease the farm labor supply elasticity, but may also reduce the support workers get from final consumers. According to a sensitivity analysis, changes in labor supply elasticity changes the buycott impact on retailers' revenue from positive to negative. This may trigger a switch from participating to not participating in the FFP, which will hurt farm workers.

Appendix

Boycott System of Equations:

$$\frac{EY}{EB} = K_X \frac{EX}{EB} + K_c \frac{Ec}{EB}$$

1-6a)

$$\frac{EP_X}{EB} = -\frac{K_c}{\sigma_Y} \frac{EX}{EB} + \frac{K_c}{\sigma_Y} \frac{Ec}{EB} + \frac{EP_Y}{EB}$$

(1-7a)

$$\frac{EP_c}{EB} = \frac{K_X}{\sigma_Y} \frac{EX}{EB} - \frac{K_X}{\sigma_Y} \frac{Ec}{EB} + \frac{EP_Y}{EB}$$

(1-8a)

$$\frac{Ec}{EB} = e_c \frac{EP_c}{EB}$$

1-9a)

$$\frac{EY}{EB} = \eta_Y \frac{EP_Y}{EB} - \frac{EB}{EB}$$

(1-10a)

$$\frac{EX}{EB} = K_L \frac{EL}{EB} + K_z \frac{Ez}{EB}$$

(1-6b)

$$\frac{EP_L}{EB} = -\frac{K_z}{\sigma_X} \frac{EL}{EB} + \frac{K_z}{\sigma_X} \frac{Ez}{EB} + \frac{EP_X}{EB}$$

(1-7b)

$$\frac{EP_z}{EB} = \frac{K_L}{\sigma_X} \frac{EL}{EB} - \frac{K_L}{\sigma_X} \frac{Ez}{EB} + \frac{EP_X}{EB}$$

(1-8b)

$$\frac{EL}{EB} = e_L \frac{EP_L}{EB}$$

(1-9b)

$$\frac{Ez}{EB} = e_z \frac{EP_z}{EB}$$

(1-10b)

Note that the system of equations includes factor shares, K_i's; factor supply elasticities, e_i; final product demand elasticity, η_Y ; and Allen elasticities of substitution (Allen elasticities), σ_Y. The K_i in Equations 1-6a through 1-8a and 1-6b through 1-8b are the relative factor shares of the inputs at each level. With linear homogeneity, the sum of the relative input shares within a level must equal one, $K_X + K_c = 1$ and $K_L + K_z = 1$.

Buycott System of Equations:

$$\frac{EY}{EV} = K_X \frac{EX}{EV} + K_c \frac{Ec}{EV}$$

$$(1\text{-}6a)$$

$$\frac{EP_X}{EV} = -\frac{K_c}{\sigma_Y}\frac{EX}{EV} + \frac{K_c}{\sigma_Y}\frac{Ec}{EV} + \frac{EP_Y}{EV} - \frac{EV}{EV}$$

$$(1\text{-}7a)$$

$$\frac{EP_c}{EV} = \frac{K_X}{\sigma_Y}\frac{EX}{EV} - \frac{K_X}{\sigma_Y}\frac{Ec}{EV} + \frac{EP_Y}{EV}$$

$$(1\text{-}8a)$$

$$\frac{Ec}{EV} = e_c \frac{EP_c}{EV}$$

$$(1\text{-}9a)$$

$$\frac{EY}{EV} = \eta_Y \frac{EP_Y}{EV}$$

$$(1\text{-}10a)$$

$$\frac{EX}{EV} = K_L \frac{EL}{EV} + K_z \frac{Ez}{EV}$$

$$(1\text{-}6b)$$

$$\frac{EP_L}{EV} = -\frac{K_z}{\sigma_X}\frac{EL}{EV} + \frac{K_z}{\sigma_X}\frac{Ez}{EV} + \frac{EP_X}{EV}$$

$$(1\text{-}7b)$$

$$\frac{EP_z}{EV} = +\frac{K_L}{\sigma_X}\frac{EL}{EV} - \frac{K_L}{\sigma_X}\frac{Ez}{EV} + \frac{EP_X}{EV}$$

$$(1\text{-}8b)$$

$$\frac{EL}{EV} = e_L \frac{EP_L}{EV} + \frac{e_L}{K_L}\frac{EV}{EV}$$

$$(1\text{-}9b)$$

$$\frac{Ez}{EV} = e_z \frac{EP_z}{EV}$$

$$(1\text{-}10b)$$

Assumed Parameter Values:

Parameter	Value	
e_c	5.00	Supply elasticity for retailer's input c
e_L	5.00	Supply elasticity for grower's input L (farmworkers)
e_z	2.00	Supply elasticity for grower's input z
σ_X	1.00	Allen elasticity at the grower's level
σ_Y	1.00	Allen elasticity at the retailer's level
η_Y	-5.00	Own price elasticity of demand
K_c	0.95	Retail level input c cost share
K_L	0.33	Grower level input L cost share
K_z	0.67	Grower level input z cost share
K_X	0.05	Retail level commodity as input cost share

Note: The demand elasticity for the retail-level products is assumed to be fairly elastic. This assumption is based on the market structure in which many retailers operate. Typically, food markets are highly competitive; the food industry has relatively no barriers to entry. According to the U.S. Census, there are 132,364 firms (under the limited service restaurant NAICS 722211) with 204,311 establishments. The number of incorporated firms under the 722211 NAICS is fairly large; according to Compustat data there are 937 of these (retrieved from http://wrds.wharton.upenn.edu/). Supply elasticities of the factors of production are also assumed to be fairly elastic based on abundant availability. In the case of farm labor, for instance, there is a continuing inflow of immigrant workers. The Allen elasticities of substitution are assumed equal to one. The share of commodities to the total cost at the retail level is assumed rather small based on the target retailers' main food inputs and operating expense information.

REFERENCES

De Pelsmacker, Patrick, Liesbeth Driesen, and Glenn Rayp. 2005. "Do Consumers Care about Ethics? Willingness to Pay for Fair Trade Coffee." *The Journal of Consumer Affairs, Vol. 39, No. 2,* 363-385.

"Fiscal Year Data for WHD." U.S. Department of Labor. Available online: https://www.dol.gov/whd/data/datatables.htm [accessed 11 March 2020].

Heyder, M., and L Theuvsen. 2012. "Determinants and Effects of Corporate Social Responsibility in German Agribusiness: A PLS Model." *Agribusiness* 400-428.

Loureiro, Maria L., and Justus Lotade. 2005. "Do Fair Trade and Eco-labels in Coffee Wake Up the Consumer Conscience?" *Econlogical Economics* 129-138.

Luhmann, H., and L. Theuvsen. 2016. "Corporate Social Responsibility in Agribusiness Literature Review and Future Research Directions." *Journal of Agricultural and Environmental Ethics* 673-696.

Mazur-Wierzbicka, E. 2015. "The Application of Corporate Social Responsibility in European Agriculture."

Monroe, Friedman. 1996. "A Positive Approach to Organized Consumer Action: The Buycott as an Alternative to the Boycott." *Journal of Consumer Policy* 439.

Owens, Colleen, Meredith Dank, Justin Breaus, Isela Bañuelos, Amy Farrell, Rebecca Pfeffer, Katie Bright, Ryan Heitsmith, and Jack McDevitt. 2014. "Understanding the Organization, Operation, and Victimization Process of Labor Trafficking in the United States." Research Report, Urban Institute and Northeastern University. Accessed June 13, 2017. https://www.ncjrs.gov/pdffiles1/nij/grants/248461.pdf.

Palacios, Jamille. 2017. "Lessons from Farmworker's Consumer Boycotts as Strategy to Address Harsh Working Conditions and Low Wage Rates." *Proceedings of the 16th Annual Conference.* Cambio Center. 53-58.

———. 2013. "Three Economic Essays on Current Farm Labor Issues ." *Dissertation.* Florida: University of Florida.

Produce Marketing Association. 2018. "PMA and United Fresh launch Ethical Charter on Responsible Labor Practices." *Fresh Fruit Portal News.* https://www.freshfruitportal.com/news/ 2018/07/12/pma-and-united-fresh-launch-ethical-charter-on-responsible-labor-practices/.

Roka, F M. 2016. "Social Accountability Coming to a Farm Near You." *The Florida Tomato Proceedings.*

Roka, F.M., and Z. Guan. 2018. "Farm Labor Management trends in Florida - Challenges and Opportunities." *International Journal of Agribusiness Management* 7 (1): 66-74.

Roka, Fritz, Derek Farnsworth, and Simnitt Skyler. 2017. "Estimating Costs of Employing Citrus Harvesters through the H-2A Guest Worker Program." *SAEA Annual Meeting.* Mobile, Alabama.

Sandovici, Maria E., and Terri Davis. 2010. "Activism Gone Shopping: An Empirical Exploration of Individual-Level Determinants of Political Consumerism and Donating." *Comparative Sociology* 328-356.

Smith, B. Gail. 2008. "Developing Sustainable Food Supply Chains." *Philosophical Transactions of Royal Society* 849-861.

Vidales, K.B.V., J.L.A. Vargas, and J.O.G. Garcia. 2012. "Exploratory Analysis fof Corporate Social Responsibility Practices in Mexican Agricultural Companies." *China-USA Business Review* 1277-1285.

CHAPTER 7

What the Halal? Islamophobia and Food Labeling in Post-9/11 U.S. Markets

Courtney I.P. Thomas (Virginia Tech)

Food labels are a direct line of communication between food producers and the public. Their function is not only to inform but to capture consumers that increasingly seek to "vote with their dollars.' In recent years, debates have raged across the United States regarding what should be included or excluded from food labels. Genetically Modified Foods? Animal growth hormones? Local? Organic? Health claims? Gluten free? Fair trade? Public agencies such as the FDA and USDA often establish the regulatory parameters for food labeling, but they are not the only institutions to do so.

For more than 80 years, organizations like the Orthodox Union have certified foods in U.S. markets that meet the demands of Jewish kosher law. The AU symbol has been called a "coveted seal of approval" by the New York Times. But of the growing number of Americans who purchase Kosher foods, only a fraction do so for religious reasons. Secular consumers cite food safety and animal welfare concerns as motivations for Kosher food purchases. That is to say, not only to most consumers not object to Kosher labeling, they embrace it beyond its religious significance. However, although Halal standards are not terribly dissimilar from their Kosher counterparts, they been received very differently by many American consumers. This chapter examines controversies surrounding Halal food labeling initiatives. It analyzes public discussions regarding Halal labeling and from those discussions explores contemporary American culture and its attitudes toward Muslim-American citizens and consumers.

HALAL STANDARDS

Halal is an Arabic word for "lawful" or "permissible" and is the opposite of *haraam*, meaning "unlawful" or "forbidden." It is used to describe foods that conform to Muslim dietary standards outlined in the Qu'ran. According to international standards elaborated by the *Codex Alimentarius Commission*, foods are considered halal except when they or their products and derivatives include:

- Pigs and boars;

- Dogs, snakes, and monkeys;
- Carnivorous animals with claws and fangs such as lions, tigers, bears, etc.;
- Birds of pretty with claws such as eagles, vultures, etc.;
- Pests such as rats, centipedes, scorpions, etc.;
- Animals forbidden to be killed in Islam including bees, ants, and woodpeckers;
- Animals considered generally repulsive such as lice, flies, maggots, etc.;
- Animals that live on both land and water such as frogs and crocodiles;
- Mules and domesticated donkeys;
- All poisonous and hazardous aquatic animals;
- All animals not slaughtered according to Islamic law;
    - The animal should be alive at the time of slaughtering;
    - The slaughtering device should be sharp and not lifted off the animal during the slaughter act;
    - The slaughter act should sever the trachea, esophagus, and main arteries and veins of the neck region;
    - The slaughterer should be a Muslim who is mentally sound and knowledgeable of the Islamic slaughtering procedures.
- Blood;
- Intoxicating and hazardous plants except where the toxin or hazard can be eliminated during processing;
- Alcoholic drinks;
- Intoxicating and hazardous drinks.[1]

WHY BUY HALAL FOOD?

In recent years, sales of Kosher certified foods have expanded well beyond the Jewish-American population. A $24 billion industry projected to grow by 11.5% by 2025, the growth of the kosher niche has outstripped other segments of the food market.[2] Among consumers who purchased Kosher foods, only 14% reported doing so for religious reasons. Many more believed the food to be of a better quality (62%), healthier (51%), or safer (34%).[3] However, when one tries to discover why consumers buy halal foods, a different picture emerges.

A 2015 Google search for "why buy halal food" turns up as its first result an article from snopes.com that evaluates the then circulating claim that "halal meat sold in the U.S. is commonly produced in conditions of filth and uncleanliness." The example email states:

[1] "General Guidelines for use of the Term "Halal,'" Codex Alimentarius Commission, accessed October 25, 2019, http://www.fao.org/docrep/005/y2770e/y2770e08.htm

[2] Jon Springer, "Kosher Food Market Set to Grow, Research Shows," Super Market News, accessed September 1, 2017, https://www.supermarketnews.com/consumer-trends/kosher-food-market-set-grow-research-shows.

[3] "3 in 5 Kosher food Buyers Purchase for Food Quality, Not Religion," Mintel, accessed February 17, 2009, http://www.mintel.com/press-centre/food-and-drink/3-in-5-kosher-food-buyers-purchase-for-food-quality-not-religion?id=321.

One of the things that halal kill plants are notorious for is putting already-dead animals in the human consumption line. They will go pick up a dead cow off of a farm or ranch and instead of putting it in their rendering tank where the resulting "tankage" is worth pennies on the dollar as pet food or industrial products, they will shackle the dead animal on the normal kill line and process it as human food which is the highest-dollar product.

Since Islam teaches dishonesty (taqiyyah) and no regard for one's neighbor, this kind of sickening behavior is standard.

Halal plants are also notorious for general citations for filth and uncleanliness. I have toured normal cattle slaughter plants, and guys, you could eat off of the floor.

Everything is white and men walk around with water hoses and steam guns constantly keeping everything in a state of spotlessness.

Halal plants are filthy. A lot of Halal meat is also labeled as "organic."[4]

Snopes responds by explaining that in 1998 the USDA recognized the potential of halal markets, both in the United States and abroad, and noted that:

Contrary to the overall declining trend in the United States' lamb, mutton, and goat consumption, there is a growing, high-value market to be found among the American Muslim population. Entrance into this particular market, as well as Muslim markets overseas, requires Halal certification.

Halal is an Islamic religious term used to describe food that is "lawful" to eat. It is similar to Kosher in the Jewish religion in many ways. Many slaughterhouses in the United States already meet the standards set by the American Muslim community for Halal status. The USDA has had a policy on Halal labeling in effect since 1996. Halal requirements are not difficult to meet, and the USDA believes that any American slaughterhouse should be able to comply with the new Halal policy.

The U.S. government is negotiating with several major Muslim countries to gain acceptance of U.S. Halal standards as equivalent to their own. This will open more markets to U.S. lamb and mutton exporters, as at least twenty Muslim countries require Halal certification for meat. There are 1.5

---

[4] David Mikkelson, "Halal Meat" Snopes, Accessed October 25, 2019, http://www.snopes.com/politics/religion/halal.asp#1QcQaY6Fr8Ig92iy.

billion Muslims throughout the world, so the potential market for Halal meat is very large.[5]

Efforts were subsequently made to harmonize U.S. halal standards with those of our trading partners in the Middle East and other countries with large Muslim populations.

But that was in 1998.

9/11 AND THE GROWTH OF ISLAMOPHOBIA IN AMERICAN CULTURE

On September 11, 2001, nineteen terrorists associated with Al Qaeda hijacked four passenger airliners. Two were flown into the World Trade Center in New York City, NY. One was flown into the Pentagon in Arlington County, VA. The fourth plane was steered toward Washington, D.C. but crashed near Shanksville, PA after passengers fought the hijackers; analysts hypothesize that it may have been headed for the Capitol building in Washington, D.C. In all, 2996 people, including the 19 hijackers, were killed.

Since 9/11 both U.S. government policies and American public opinion have institutionalized and perpetuated fear, and often outright hatred, of Muslims in the United States and around the world. A 2010 Gallup survey reported that sixty percent of Americans believed that their fellow countrymen are prejudiced against Muslim-Americans.[6] Just under half of American Muslims report that they have, personally, experienced racial or religious discrimination in 2010.

But even peripheral glimpses into American culture suggest that those numbers are far too low.

No one wants to be called a racist or a bigot. We've come far enough as a culture, not to eradicate prejudice and hate, but to force those who spew them to attempt to mask them as something else.

Sometimes.

In the aftermath of 9/11 and the War on Terror, it has become more socially acceptable to profess anti-Muslim opinions and ideas, particularly if they are prefaced by, "Now, I'm not a racist, but…" or "I don't think *all* Muslims are terrorists but…" When your government profiles Muslim-Americans for increased scrutiny in airports, sends tens of thousands of soldiers to die in a War on Terror that the general public cannot differentiate from a War on Islam, and the President enacts a ban on travelers from predominantly Muslim countries, the barriers to Islamophobia are eroded and often washed away. Like African-Americans after the Civil War and Japanese-Americans after Pearl Harbor, an American is unlikely to be called out for being anti-Muslim in post 9/11 America. Beyond this, the proliferation of online discussion boards since 9/11 gives those who would profess

---

[5] *Ibid.*
[6] "Islamophobia: Understanding Anti-Muslim Sentiment in the West," Gallup, accessed March 14, 2018, http://www.gallup.com/poll/157082/islamophobia-understanding-anti-muslim-sentiment-west.aspx.

anti-Muslim beliefs an outlet, often one shrouded in anonymity, for unambiguous, unfiltered, and unapologetic vitriol.

THE PROBLEM WITH DORITOS™

In 2008, consumers dedicated to complying with Muslim dietary standards discovered that Dorito™ chips marketed by the Frito Lay corporation, which had been sold in many halal grocery stores, were, in fact, haraam. This caused an uproar in many Muslim-American communities, though it is important to note that the chips were not certified halal by a third-party certifier (TPC) nor were they marketed by Frito Lay, a division of PepsiCo, as halal; they were merely assumed to be halal by merchandisers and consumers. The problem was the presence of alcohol used as a flavor carrier in the chips topping. Alcohol, of course, is strictly prohibited by Muslim dietary law.

The uproar extended beyond the Muslim-American community as many American consumers became aware, many for the first time, that foods that conformed to Muslim dietary standards were part of mainstream American cuisine and often enjoyed well beyond that niche community. When the story was "seeded" to MSNBC's social news site, Newsvine, the comments included:

> Sandie Seward AUTHORFeb 22, 2008
> Well, this just about tops the lot , the hard-line Muslims have really excelled themselves this time

> Gwenny Feb 22, 2008
> Maybe we need to institute the death penalty for such extreme stupidity. Or at least mandatory sterilization. SHEESH even Muslim scholars declared the chips safe, what the hell do these people want?

> Sandie Seward AUTHORFeb 24, 2008
> Dennis, Walkers are not offending a "large part of their customer base." In actual fact, the only ones they are "offending" are the radical hotheads that are looking for any little thing to cause trouble over.

> space guy Feb 24, 2008
> This is not bigotry, this is people being tired of having to change our culture to meet the needs of newly immigrating people. If you don't like living somewhere you don't have to stay. So just put a sock in your accusations.[7]

---

[7]"Breaking News & top Stories-Latest World, US & Local News," NBC News, Accessed October 25, 2019, http://seward.newsvine.com/_news/2008/02/22/1319079-furious-muslims-criticies-walkers-crisps-for-their-alcohol-content#th223674-c1505714.

This was my first insight into a subgroup of Americans whose hatred and intolerance for Muslims extended to what they chose to eat. It was not my last.

BACK TO THE SEARCH FOR "WHY BUY HALAL FOOD?"

The Snopes article is immediately followed by several links to halal food distributors. Then there is an article from the Daily Mail, a UK publication that explains that millions of consumers throughout the UK eat halal food without knowing it as major food processors embrace halal standards so that their food can be eaten by Muslims and non-Muslims alike.

But is it okay for a Christian to eat halal food?

For the answer, you need only click a few links down. There gotquestions.org, a website that promises to answer questions about God, Jesus, the Bible, or theology that describes itself as a "para-church ministry" designed to "help people find answers to their spiritually related questions," answers just that.[8] It explains that the "problem comes when Allah's name is pronounced over the meat during the butchering process" because "many interpret this to mean that the animal was sacrificed to a false god—an idol."[9]

Despite the fact that the organization's statement of faith declares that it believes in "one God, who is the creator of all," and that the "Bible, comprised of the Old and New Testaments, [is] the inspired, infallible, and authoritative World of God, it ignores the fact that "Allah" is the Arabic name for the *same one God* of the Old and New Testaments, a God that it acknowledges goes by many names.[10] It concludes, "if we are with others who believe that halal food is wrong to eat, we should refrain out of concern for their conviction. If we are served food by someone who makes a point that it is halal, we should refrain as a quiet sign that we do not accept the authority of the false god to which it was dedicated. If we are in a restaurant or market or school or home that, we suspect, is serving halal food, we should eat and give thanks to the true God who provides."[11]

But how do Americans feel about growing efforts on the part of producers and processors to ensure that their products conform to halal standards?

The last link on the first page of search results takes us to barenakedislam.com, a site that proclaims that "it isn't Islamophobia when they really ARE trying to kill you." An article titled "Are you inadvertently supporting Islamic terrorism by unwittingly buying halal food" explains to consumers how they can tell if the food they are eating is halal certified or not. What it doesn't do is demonstrate any linkage whatsoever between halal certified foods and the funding of terrorist organizations. Nor does it explain that the certifying agencies are working for mainstream food producers and processors that operate in an oligopolistic market in which a dozen agribusinesses control nearly the entirety of U.S. food sales. The article explains that Campbell's Soup contracts with the Islamic Society of North

---

[8] "About," GotQuestions (2004) http://www.gotquestions.org/about.html.
[9] "Halal Food," GotQuestions (2004) http://www.gotquestions.org/halal-food.html.
[10] "Faith" GotQuestions (2004), http://www.gotquestions.org/faith.html.
[11] "Halal Food," GotQuestions (2004) http://www.gotquestions.org/halal-food.html.

America to certify some of its product lines as halal compliant. They maintain that the ISNA funnels money from its certifying operations to Hamas and calls on consumers to "let [Campbell's] know that you will never purchase their products as long as they choose to submit to halal certification and certainly if they choose to go halal in America."[12] Note below that it refers to this funding as a "hidden tax" because you'll "never find the numbers."

ISNA is an organization that seeks to strengthen and develop Muslim American communities and enhance interfaith collaboration and civic engagement. It publicly rejects terrorism and violence and calls it the epitome of injustice, but was listed by the US government as an indicted co-conspirator in a terrorism case regarding the Israeli/Palestinian dispute. This indictment is cited by barenakedislam as the reason for its condemnation of Campbell's, but the site does not provide context about the organization or its ties to Hamas or other organizations. Instead, it allows its readers to reach their own conclusions.

And they do.

Undoubtedly already a self-selecting group, commenters on this article expressed the following ideas. Note how the site administrators are quick to extol the virtues of Kosher food while demonizing halal. Comments here included are unedited and unabridged, mistakes, lies, intolerance, and all.

> **Jodi APRIL 20, 2015** @ 7:33 PM
> Can anyone please help me find out more information as to why a skin care product I'm using and selling to other states on the box that it is Certified HALAL. It also states it's made in the USA. What's this mean?

> **BareNakedIslam APRIL 20, 2015** @ 8:14 PM
> It means it is Islamic-approved with no alcohol or pork products in it. And it was prayed over by a filthy imam. Take it back to the store and return it telling them you don't want to buy Islamic products, part of which goes toward supporting Islamic terrorism

> **Anti-Islam APRIL 18, 2015** @ 4:19 PM
> Greetings. Is there any website that will inform me to boycott products that are halal? Because, I am against buying anything that is halal. Thank you.

> **BareNakedIslam APRIL 18, 2015** @ 5:57 PM
> This site has a very comprehensive list by country: http://www. zabihah.com

> **Anti-Islam APRIL 18, 2015** @ 9:21 PM
> Thank you very much for the website. It is very informative. There is a Turkish restaurant in Boston and the food is very delicious. I went there

---

[12]"Are You Inadvertently Supporting Islamic Terrorism by Unwittingly Buying Halal Food?" BareNakedIslam (2013) http://www.barenakedislam.com/2013/03/29/are-you-inadvertently-supporting-islamic-terrorism-by-unwittingly-buying-halal-food/.

few many times. I found out tonight on the website that you posted and I have read that the restaurant serves halal foods and it shocked me. I did not realize that the Turkish restaurant serves halal food. Now, I do not want to go there, anymore, because they serve halal food that supports Islamic terrorism and I do not want to pay anything halal that supports Islamic terrorism. Therefore, I kiss that Turkish restaurant in Boston good-bye, forever.

BareNakedIslam APRIL 18, 2015 @ 9:32 PM
Every restaurant from a muslim based country serves only halal.

Anti-Islam **APRIL 18, 2015** @ 9:58 PM
I do believe that restaurants that are Muslim-owned serve only halal food. i prefer to stay away from them.

Allan Ivarsson NSW Australia - "No Islam!" **MARCH 5, 2015** @ 4:31 PM
N.B.
You are a liar and a fool, clearly you are Muslim. BNI is not spreading hate; BNI is tabling truth. In fact if you look closely, BNI is posting reports and statements made by thousands of people around the world constantly against Islam.
I read the Koran in 1984 and I don't need BNI or any other person to tell me that the Koran is an evil violent book. I saw that fact with my own eyes. The Koran texts are riddled with "Hate Speech'.
Millions of us against Islam have read the insidious Koran texts.
You need to learn from ex-Muslims that were smart enough to dump Islam.

Baldino Bingg FEBRUARY 26, 2015 @ 10:28 PM
Don't want to pay a halal tax to muzzie scum, also don't want to pay a kosher tax as I don't care if the food is kosher. Please don't let the blind hatred obscure the fact that both "certifications" are a shakedown.

BareNakedIslam FEBRUARY 26, 2015 @ 11:08 PM
You're full of crap. Nobody is forcing businesses to carry Kosher food, muslims are forcing halal on businesses, part of which goes to fund terrorism. If you live in Australia or the UK, virtually all your meat is halal. Hardly any is kosher and it's always marked. Halal is force-fed to ignorant Westerers, often without being marked. Don't post here again or I will ban you.
Jim Mitchell **JANUARY 9, 2014** @ 12:42 PM
"In Rome do as the Romans." In America, do as the Americans. Islamic people need to raise their animals to slaughter as needed under their law. If not, stay in an Islamic country that practices your beliefs dictated by their government. How can we respect a religion who dices their women and

treats them like dirt under the men's feet. LOL...keep the women covered because of their inferiority to their awesome men counterparts!!!

BareNakedIslam NOVEMBER 10, 2013 @ 5:29 PM
ww, you are wrong:
Kosher vs. Halal:
Kosher – requires the animal be slaughtered quickly and humanely, strictly forbidding cruel slow methods like strangulation.
Halal – requires the animal be bled out in agony while sick people who get off watching that kind of thing have a "festival."
Kosher – requires the blood be drained cleanly from the *carcass* of the humanely killed animal, removing toxins released from cells into the bloodstream at the moment of death from the meat.
Halal –leaves the meat *filled* with toxins released at the moment of death because the blood is removed while the animal is dying and therefore is not present in sufficient quantities to remove those last toxins.
Kosher – contains little to no cortisol or norepenepherine (two stress chemicals that are similar enough from mammal to mammal to cross species) because the animal to be killed is treated well before it is put down and is generally not frightened as it is put down (because in a truly kosher slaughter situation, animals cannot be slaughtered in a sequential fashion, as the waste of one could contaminate the next, so they are not exposed to the "scent of death" the way non-kosher culls are)
Halal – animals watch other animals die during the blood letting festival, smelling their fear and raising their own stress. These stress chemicals "marinate" the meat in hormones known to raise levels of aggression and violence in nearly all mammal species (including human).
Kosher – requires cooking the cleanly drained meat completely, cooking any remaining stress chemicals into oblivion.
Halal – allows for a surprising range of cooking methods, including even some "tar tar" dishes (raw or nearly raw), allowing for the spread of disease and chemicals and hormones that were not removed by the idiotic slow bloodletting practice and half-measure cooking.
Kosher – the spinal cord is sectioned thus cutting off pain to the brain. Therefore, no suffering or terror.
Halal – spinal cord left intact.

SaveChristianity **JULY 26, 2013** @ 2:25 PM
Through the halal taxes we are unknowingly funding the destruction of America.

Ernie **MAY 12, 2013** @ 8:29 AM
I saw a new display of Halal chicken in a cooler case at a local Superstore. That store staff must not have been very well indoctrinated since immediately adjacent to the display was a section packed full of packaged hams. Did I pick up some of the hams to check the price and accidentally

put them down in the halal display? I can't remember but it might hav happened that way.

***Billy* APRIL 9, 2013** @ 10:45 AM
I just checked a can of Campbell's Cream of Chicken & Mushroom soup that's been in my cabinet and there was that symbol (second row extreme right) on the can. It's so well disguised, a bunch of scrambled figures,tiny, black and white that I never would have noticed it without the list of symbols, so thank you for the list. Now, off to the trash to throw that filthy can out.

***ADHD* MARCH 31, 2013** @ 1:40 AM
Well done, dear Ms. BNI!!!!!
Yesterday, when I was in the supermarket, I noticed one of those symbol-tags (second row, extremest right) present on several products. I'm very glad NOT to have bought any of those things. That particular symbol-tag is especially INSIDIOUS: you can't tell what it's saying (in any lettering), but it sure resembles some of the bar-code imagery (itself unnerving to not a few people). It's quite generic so most people who don't know it will end up at the minimum paying the "halal" tax if not really buy real "halal"-produce!!!!
The third "logo" from the top also apparently appeared on a container of maple-syrup (the "M' inside the gibbous moon, with the black crescent on the left) – which caused me not to buy that product either!!!
Here's hoping you had a Blessed Passover and are now having a happy Easter-time – MANY, MANY, MANY thanks for this posting!!!!
DEATH TO ISLAM – and all other totalitarianism – now, forever and unto ages of ALL ages, Amen!!!!!

***Ronyvo* MARCH 30, 2013** @ 4:27 AM
Here is a horrific thought. I am, actually, surprised that they (Muslims) did not poisen the foods they export to the infidels..Do you think that this is crazy idea?!

***SarahSue* MARCH 30, 2013** @ 3:36 AM
I am very angry to find that Cabot cheese, V8 and Pepsi have halal certification. I swore off halal about ten years ago, when I became aware of it.
It really burns my chaps to know that I have been eating it unknowingly. Lots and lots of thank for bringing this to my attention. Now I need to throw up because I ate some Cabot cheese for dinner. Ugh! SarahSue

***Allan Ivarsson NSW Australia - "No Islam!"* MARCH 30, 2013** @ 12:10 AM
BNI is this hidden Halal Tax operational in USA or around the globe? I would like to learn more detail of how it works. This "Halal' thing is

becoming a "Jihad nightmare' and Muslims are using it head-on as a weapon against us to Islamize the Globe. Governments and many CEO's are just submitting to their demands. I vaguely think I heard that a McDonald's head-office manager said that the Halal branch decision is made by franchise's not head-office; this seemed to be an ostrich cop-out response. We are going to have to rethink strategy to beat this madness. Boycotting is necessary but it won't stop all the ignorant fools from buying halal products that refuse to learn the dark truth about Islam. I wonder if Christians should create their own label and demand it be placed on all food? That demand would really put pressure on CEO's and Government's- to refuse such a demand would be descrimination.

BareNakedIslam MARCH 30, 2013 @ 2:26 AM
ALLAN, you'll never find it spelled out in monetary terms, that's why I call it the hidden halal tax. Halal production and certification costs money, above and beyond the actual cost of the item. It is passed on from the halal producers to the purveyors to the customers and a certain amount goes back to the costs of trying to Islamize the world, as CAIR and its affiliated Muslim Brotherhood groups are doing from within each country. No way to know much gets into the hands of terrorists. Muslims like to say, the first step in getting non-muslims to accept sharia is to get it into their food supply.
The most dangerous aspect of this, at least in the USA, is that the FDA does not require halal to be labeled as such. On those 2 websites listed above, you'll find products that are halal but you won't necessarily know it by looking at the package. Butterball never put a halal stamp on their turkeys, it was only on their website but as soon as it got so much negative publicity, via the internet backlash, they simply scrubbed their website of any reference to halal. Then lied and said that only the birds they send overseas are halal.

Beans MARCH 30, 2013 @ 5:36 AM
Muslims like to say, the first step in getting non-muslims to accept sharia is to get it into their food supply.
This is so true, and many don't realize just how far this has come. Specially in australia. Not sure in other countrys but it would nearly be the same at a guess.

Metron MARCH 29, 2013 @ 9:03 PM
We must begin to ask about the products we buy contain traces of halal meat. I know that halal meat is mixed with regular meat and sold without any labeling, so there is a high risk to get halal meat without knowing it. We should avoid all food that contains even small traces of halal.

Ort MARCH 29, 2013 @ 8:03 PM

Oh man! I didn't know that about Campbell's and Pepsi and Cadbury!! Does that mean ALL their products are halal? I do remembering going to a grocery store by me, and they just started switching half it's chicken case to halal. I complained. I told the ignorant foreign guy working there if this halal crap was staying. He looked at me like I had 3 heads. Filthy, foreign owned grocery store. I will only buy a couple types of veggies there, as I can't find ther like anywhere else. I will buy all my meat elsewhere.

FOOD AID FOR REFUGEES

Lest we be tempted to think that it is only a self-selecting audience on a site whose denials of Islamophobia make us think it doth protest too much and serves only to reinforce that clear ideological commitment, let us look at a 2015 article on Political Insider that reported on an advocacy group that petitioned to ensure that food aid include cultural appropriate, including halal, food. In recent years, more and more refugees from the war-torn regions of the Middle East and North Africa, especially Somalia, have relocated to the American Midwest under political asylum and refugee agreements. Food shelves in Minneapolis have a historical dearth of halal foods but a group of Somali women, Isuroon, formed a local nonprofit designed to enhance the health and empowerment of Somali women. They asked the city to allocate $150,000 to fund a new food shelf for kosher or halal foods.[13]

That's not how Political Insider spun the story. It reported that "an Islamic women's "advocacy group' is DEMANDING a county in Minnesota change its food stamp policies to require a low-price halal food shelf."[14] It maintained that "coming to America poor, they receive unlimited health services, free transportation, free housing, and children receive free education. In addition to halal food, gratitude is also in short supply."[15]

Comments on the article dripped of references to majoritarian American culture and xenophobia and included:

Millie says: July 30, 2015 at 11:14 pm
Religious beliefs. Buy dried beans and don't put pork in them. It's not that hard to figure out. Dang put forth some kind of effort to support yourself. My tax dollars are for AMERICANS that need it and have earned it.

Wayne says: July 30, 2015 at 9:39 pm

---

[13] Cirien Saadeh, "South Minneapolis Somali Community Asks for Ethnic, Healthy Food Shelf," Twin City Daily Planet (2015), http://www.tcdailyplanet.net/south-minneapolis-somali-community-asks-ethnic-healthy-food-shelf/.
[14] Patrick Fye, "Food Stamps: Muslims Demand Welfare Be Free of Pork for Islamic Halal Diet," Inquisitr, Accessed November 13, 2019, https://www.inquisitr.com/1555325/food-stamps-muslims-demand-welfare-be-free-of-pork-for-islamic-diet-video/.
[15] *Ibid.*

Who are they to demand anything!!!! I'll bet most of these Muslims never contributed a dime to the system,now they want even more.If they don't like the food they're getting with the food stamps then GET THE HELL OUT OF OUR COUNTRY!!!!!!

Sara says: July 30, 2015 at 11:14 am
I am SO fed up with the different ethnic groups that come to this country and then DEMAND we give them special rights/privileges. IF, you want to come to this country for it's freedoms; then you need to embrace OUR way of life. If we were to go to their country and DEMAND such rights/privileges; we would be jailed or killed. Any officer of the U.S. government (county, state or federal) that gives in to any of these demands, should be stripped of his job because he/she is not upholding OUR constitution. You came here for a reason, so get over yourselves and live like Americans or go the hell back where you came from. 99.9% of true AMERICANS actually prefer that you DO LEAVE and tell all your friends back home how un-accommodating we are; therefore no one else from your country will come here.

Ricky says: July 30, 2015 at 9:38 am
The community of Muslim's here in the Twin Cities is HUGE. Why don't these Muslims get together and take care of it themselves. Go home if you ungrateful S.O.B.S think your being mistreated. I live in MPLS and I can tell you from experience, they are ungrateful and hateful toward Minnesotans and the American people.

Tony says: July 10, 2015 at 11:01 pm
As an American I say send the terroist trash back to their own country and let them mooch off of their goverment.

Carla says: July 9, 2015 at 11:34 pm
If you hate Western civilization and 99.9% of you hate America and Americans, stop sponging off of our country and move back to your middle eastern countries. Give the food stamps to people who LOVE our great nation. Go away.

Jay says:July 9, 2015 at 7:43 pm
Go Away

Lisa says:July 9, 2015 at 6:19 pm
2 choices GET A JOB but preferably GO HOME,,,!!!

Linda says:July 9, 2015 at 4:28 pm
Why do you come here looking for handouts? Can't you or your husband get a job? you guys are milking America dry!! Don't eat pork? That is not our problem!! You can go fishing or hunting!!!!

John says:July 9, 2015 at 1:13 am
Oh man…this is funny, but ridiculous. They think they will get what they want because the president is a Muslim. Can't wait for Donald Trump to be the president, he will kick their ass and send them back where they come from. Okay, I'll try to be generous. I will donate a halal pig but if they will refuse to eat, they will be beheaded.

Roberta says: June 11, 2015 at 7:43 pm
invite them to a PIG ROAST! If they're offended put them on a leaky boat back to where they can have their own food. Problem is they will have to work for it,oh no,not that! They do not belong here.

Scott says: June 11, 2015 at 5:49 pm
Go make demands in your own country you stupid Muslim idiots.

Harold says: June 11, 2015 at 11:36 am
Your Muslim Leader will do what he can as quick as he can. We don't want you ragheads to feel left out, In the mean time try a bacon wrapped pizza from Little Ceasers.

Mary says: June 10, 2015 at 11:28 pm
These muslums are geting our goverment to pay for there food when they dont even deserve to be here.I never thought id feel this way about muslums,but there over here trying to get food for free and just take from us the people!!! We the people want them going back to there country!!

Chris Lee says: June 10, 2015 at 9:56 pm
Is there any way we can get these people out of our country?

Irish says: May 23, 2015 at 1:03 pm
These muzzie women need to get the hell out of my country,we dont go to the middle east and demand a certain food be available to us,tis bad enough people consume animals but thats another story for another time,food banks do not and will not ever cater to certain ethic groups,take wot is offered and be thankful,stupid ignorant muzzies!

Anita says: May 23, 2015 at 12:09 pm
HELLO…..you live in America, you eat American. Period. Can't be choosy when we provide the food for FREE! If not, move back home. We don't want your cultures in America so adjust to ours or leave!

Michael says: May 22, 2015 at 11:44 pm
IF THESE TERRORISTS WANT US AS REAL AMERICANS TO BEND TO THEIR DEMANDS,THEN THEY SHOULD BEND TO ALL OF OUR DEMANDS,LIKE NOT WEARING HEAD RAGS OF ANYKIND TO HIDE THEIR FACES,ABIDE BY THE CONSTITUTION

OF NTHIS COUNTRY AND DENOUNCE THE PIG LOVEING COUNTRY THEY CAME FROM,THAT OR GET THE HELL OUT OF MY COUNTRY!!!!!!!!!!!!!!!!!!!!!!

SCHOOL LUNCHES

Anita says, if "you live in America, you eat American." But what does it mean to eat "American"?

The least common denominator of American food has to be the typical public school lunch. Subsidized by the USDA, school lunches are replete with chicken nuggets, cheeseburgers, fish sticks, hot dogs, pizza, corn dogs, or slabs of overcooked meat, often fried and dripping with gravy, with fried potato products, overcooked vegetables, and processed fruit in high fructose corn syrup on the side and chocolate or strawberry milk, fruit punch, or soda to drink. Efforts made by the Obama administration to transform school lunches to include whole grains, fresh vegetables, and low fat dairy were met with resistance from schools throughout the country, and were ultimately abandoned and rolled back by the Trump administration.

In September 2008, a principal from a Portland, Oregon school incorporated food into the school system's equity program, an initiative designed to foster diversity and cultural acceptance among students. He pondered the "subtle language of racism" at work in classrooms and lunchrooms when he asked of a teacher who had used the peanut butter sandwich as an example in a lesson, "what about Somali or Hispanic students, who might not eat sandwiches?"[16]

But majoritarian cultural biases are apparent even in his observations. He goes on to say, "Another way [to teach] would be to say: "Americans eat peanut butter and jelly. Do you have anything like that?' Let them tell you. Maybe they eat torta. Or pita."

The story was repeated across the country and, as is common in the digital game of telephone that is modern online media, was blown completely out of proportion by the time it reached the attention of many Americans. Headlines screamed, "Is Portland Schools Spending Half a Million Dollars to Declare the Peanut-Butter-and-Jelly Sandwich Racist?"

The answer, quite demonstrably, is no. In fact, after investigating the claim, Politifact Oregon rated the statement "pants on fire."[17] For while the entire budget of the equity program between 2007 and the incident in 2008 had come in around a half million dollars, the principal's PBJ initiative (if one can even categorize a statement made at a faculty meeting as such) is but one part of a larger movement. Furthermore, the principal never actually called the sandwich racist.

But she was onto something. Research suggests that children who do not see the foods they eat at home represented on the school menu may feel alienated from

---

[16]Janie Har, "Is Portland Schools Spending Half a Million Dollars to Declare the Peanut-Butter-and-Jelly-Sandwich Racist?" Politifact, accessed November 13, 2019, http://www.politifact.com/oregon/statements/2012/sep/18/education-action-group/portland-schools-spending-half-million-dollars-dec/.
[17]*Ibid.*

both schools and classmates. They may be hesitant to invite classmates into their homes. They may be embarrassed by their families or cultures and seek to reject one or both in the name of assimilation with mainstream culture. Surely our school systems could go a long way toward global education if they not only talked about different foods but served them as part of their lunch programs. Putting aside for a moment the potential nutritional benefits of more diverse lunch offerings, the social benefits of cultural awareness on the part of majoritarian students and cultural validation on the part of minority and migrant students could go a long way toward promoting mutual respect. Vandana Shiva's research elaborates on the West's cultural attachments to white food as signs of supremacism, purity, elitism, and privilege.

Yet, once again, the comments on the right-wing news sites that covered the story, veered toward the racist, elitist, exceptionalist, and, despite the fact that the article had nothing to do with Muslim-Americans, even the Islamophobic:

> **Holdmynose** • 3 years ago
> The "white codes of behavior" have made the US an extremely successful nation which is distinctly different from the very cultures and circumstances that immigrants fled from. The schools should be promoting the American way

> **Rose Thompson** Holdmynose • 2 years ago
> Exactly! It was at one time thatnother cultures came to America to become American, to assimilate. Now they want to leave and simply resettle here. Roosevelt warned us of this in 1907- ...butvthis is predicated upon the person's becoming in every facet an American, and nothing but an American.

> **mrminwnc** • 3 years ago
> oh, FFS. every time i hear/read about how we ought to encourage different cultures to flourish in this country I want to ask these idiots: "How about we take a look at how well that culture has succeeded in their homeland?" And if we see that their homeland still aspires to achieve the status of a 3rd world festering s***hole- as they almost invariably do- then the proper response is, "Thanks, but whaddaya say we do it the American way, you know, as long as we're in AMERICA? You want to have YOUR CULTURE supported? Fine, go back to YOUR COUNTRY."

> **ishallbefree** • 3 years ago
> It's bull$hit like this that makes the Klan seem reasonable...

> **Aaron Brown** • 2 years ago
> "What about Somali or Hispanic students, who might not eat sandwiches.......UMMM REALLY????The sandwich was just a medifore, obviously the teacher used something he was familiar and comfortable with, and something most of the kids would be familiar with .. Since we do

live in the USA, and not MEXICO, thus far...IF he was a mexican teacher, mabey he would have used a TACO for an example. Would you label HIM a racist for using taco instead of pb&j????YOu know, I see an awful large amount of disrespectful, and ungrateful Immigrants/illegal immigrant kids, that grew up here in the USA, and made this country their home. Why do you live here? If you have such a problem with the USA, go the hell back to the country you or your parents came from. Fly your mexican, jewish, Italian, japanese, muslim, and african flaggs, but just remember where you raise your kids, and lay your heads every night....... Right Here in THE USA.... God BLess America.....[18]

Conclusion

As I was researching and writing, suffocating under the venomous hatred spewed by my countrymen, by the complete lack of perspective and empathy and basic human compassion, I was asked by a graduate student, "why does any of this matter?"[19]

It should certainly matter to anyone interested in the pervasiveness of hatred and ethnocentrism and majoritarian culture and xenophobia and racism in the United States.

And it matters to me, as an educator, undergraduate advisor, and orientation leader at Virginia Tech, where this very issue hit a little too close to home in the summer of 2019. On August 14, 2019, Penny Nance, President and CEO of Concerned Women for America, "the nation's largest public-policy women's organization with a rich history of more than 30 years of helping our members across the country bring Biblical principles into all levels of public policy," took to The Federalist to complain that her son's orientation at my institution was "full of leftist propaganda."[20] Among her many grievances with the university's orientation program, she cited the food provided to students and their families as one of the mechanisms of indoctrination, an alarming and shocking assault on conservative value and people. "Interestingly," she wrote, "the university offered Halal food but no certified kosher meals. Religiously observant Jewish students, tough luck, but if you are a vegan, you're in business."

Ignoring the slight against a university whose food system has consistently ranked as the best in the country, there was a dog-whistle implication to her complaint, an implication that the group she referred to as "simply...American college student[s]" would have no need for Halal foods. Identity politics, indeed, but not all identities. "We all have rights, too."[21]

---

[18]"Portland Schools Spend $500k to Deem PB&J Sandiwches Racist," Breitbart, accessed November 13, 2019, http://www.breitbart.com/big-government/2012/09/16/portland-oregon-schools-spent-526-901-to-learn-that-pb-j-sandiwches-are-racist/.
[19] Thank you, Alec Clott.
[20] Penny Nance, "My Son's Freshman Orientation at Virginia Tech was Full of Leftist Propaganda," The Federalist, accessed November 13, 2019, https://thefederalist.com/2019/08/14/sons-freshman-orientation-virginia-tech-full-leftist-propaganda/.
[21] *Ibid.*

But what does this say to an audience of food scholars?

Here's what I decided: Food should be a bridge between cultures, the gateway to the unknown. By breaking bread with those who are different from us, we learn more about them and ourselves, their culture and our own. Food is the most common denominator of human civilization, but it is also the most diverse in its expressions and manifestations. Food allows us to learn from each other.

When I was in graduate school, I befriended a Turkish student. She was my first Turkish friend, my first Muslim friend, and despite our cultural differences, we found in one another kindred souls. When she cooked for me incredible Turkish meals, the peasant and comfort foods on which she had been raised, she gave me a piece of herself, she bequeathed to me a piece of her history, her family, her culture. She taught me to stuff grape leaves with rice cooked with garlic and lemon juice, to make the perfectly proportioned cup of tea with a Turkish teapot, to properly eat hummus and baklava. Stews and salads and appetizers and desserts, I have Celiac disease, and she made them all gluten free. That wasn't her custom, but her willingness to modify her family recipes was one of the greatest expressions of love I've known, and as we sat together around her table we became family. And when my husband and I cooked chili and hamburgers and roast turkeys and other recipes from our families, when we invited her home with us to eat with those families around their own tables, we sealed bonds of friendship that neither time nor distance can erase. She ate my mother's strawberry jelly smeared liberally over my grandmother's homemade biscuits. She ate heirloom tomatoes and cucumbers from my grandmother's garden and explained how her family would serve them with olive oil, vinegar, and herbs. We learned from each other, shared the best of each other, and now when my grandmother and parents think of Muslims, they don't think of terrorists, and they don't react with fear or hatred. They think of Terken, sitting at the table, drinking sweet tea, and eating strawberry shortcake.

Food should bring us together, not divide us. It should transcend our own cultural attachments to let us experience sensations in new and exciting ways. It should push the boundaries of what we know and create something more than the sum of its parts.

When we discuss food in terms of "us" and "them," when we make cultural acceptance, let alone citizenship, the exclusive privilege of those who eat hamburgers and hot dogs instead of pita and lamb stew, when we "invite" refugees fleeing war and unthinkable violence to a pig roast knowing full well that the consumption of pork is prohibited by cultural and religious tradition, we diminish ourselves and everything that we have to offer as a society.

Pita or croissant or baguette, naan or bagel or biscuit, anpan or arepa or brotchen, bretzel or challah or tortilla, let us break bread together and share in the bountiful harvest of the cultures of the world. And let us label our foods in ways that expand our markets and communities, imaginations and empathy, connections and inclusion. Instead of asking, "Why does this matter?" let what is so dearly important to some be, by extension, important to us all.

REFERENCES

Bare Naked Islam. "Are You Inadvertently Supporting Islamic Terrorism by Unwittingly Buying Halal Food?" BARE NAKED ISLAM, March 29, 2013. http://www.barenakedislam.com/2013/03/29/are-you-inadvertently-supporting-islamic-terrorism-by-unwittingly-buying-halal-food/.

Education Action Group. "Portland Schools Spend $500k to Deem PB&J Sandwiches Racist." Breitbart, September 16, 2012. http://www.breitbart.com/big-government/2012/09/16/portland-oregon-schools-spent-526-901-to-learn-that-pb-j-sandwiches-are-racist/.

Frye, Parick. "Food Stamps: Muslims Demand Welfare Be Free of Pork for Islamic Halal Diet?" Inquisitr, accessed November 13, 2019, https://www.inquisitr.com/1555325/food-stamps-muslims-demand-welfare-be-free-of-pork-for-islamic-diet-video/.

Gallup. "Islamophobia: Understanding Anti-Muslim Sentiment in the West." Gallup.com. Gallup, March 14, 2018. http://www.gallup.com/poll/157082/islamophobia-understanding-anti-muslim-sentiment-west.aspx.

GENERAL GUIDELINES FOR USE OF THE TERM "HALAL". Codex Alimentarius Commission. Accessed October 25, 2019. http://www.fao.org/docrep/005/y2770e/y2770e08.htm.

GotQuestions.org. "About GotQuestions.org." GotQuestions.org, April 4, 2004. http://www.gotquestions.org/about.html.

———. "Statement of Faith." GotQuestions.org, April 4, 2004. http://www.gotquestions.org/faith.html.

———. "What Are the Different Names of God, and What Do They Mean?" GotQuestions.org, February 13, 2007. http://www.gotquestions.org/names-of-God.html.

———. "Is It Allowable for a Christian to Eat Halal Food?" GotQuestions.org, March 16, 2011. http://www.gotquestions.org/halal-food.html.

Harr, Janie. "Is Portland Schools Spending Half a Million Dollars to Declare the Peanut-Butter-and-Jelly Sandwich Racist?" *PolitiFact*, September 12, 2012. http://www.politifact.com/oregon/statements/2012/sep/18/education-action-group/portland-schools-spending-half-million-dollars-dec/.

Mikkelson, David. "Halal Meat." Snopes.com. Accessed October 25, 2019. http://www.snopes.com/politics/religion/halal.asp#1QcQaY6Fr8Ig92iy.

Mintel. "3 In 5 Kosher Food Buyers Purchase for Food Quality, Not Religion." February 17, 2009. http://www.mintel.com/press-centre/food-and-drink/3-in-5-kosher-food-buyers-purchase-for-food-quality-not-religion?id=321.

Nance, Penny. "My Son's Orientation At Virginia Tech Was Full Of Leftist Propaganda." The Federalist, August 19, 2019. https://thefederalist.com/2019/08/14/sons-freshman-orientation-virginia-tech-full-leftist-propaganda/.

NBCNews. "Breaking News & Top Stories - Latest World, US & Local News." NBC News. NBC. Accessed October 25, 2019. http://seward.newsvine.com/_news/2008/02/22/1319079-furious-muslims-criticies-walkers-crisps-for-their-alcohol-content#th223674-c1505714.

Saadeh, Cirien. "South Minneapolis Somali Community Asks for Ethnic, Healthy Food Shelf." Twin Cities Daily Planet, August 17, 2015. http://www.tcdailyplanet.net/south-minneapolis-somali-community-asks-ethnic-healthy-food-shelf/.

Springer, Jon. "Kosher Food Market Set to Grow, Research Shows." Supermarket News, September 1, 2017. https://www.supermarketnews.com/consumer-trends/kosher-food-market-set-grow-research-shows.

www.ingramcontent.com/pod-product-compliance
Lightning Source LLC
Chambersburg PA
CBHW052012030426
42334CB00029BA/3189